PLAYTIME
activity book

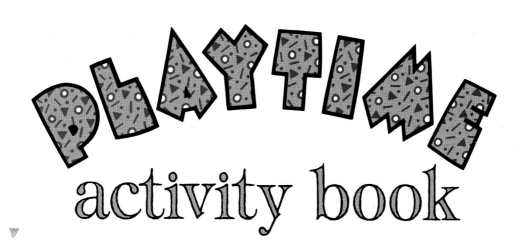

PLAYTIME
activity book

Edited by
SARA STRANGE

BBC BOOKS

Cover illustration by Kate Simpson

Published by BBC Books,
a division of BBC Enterprises Limited,
Woodlands, 80 Wood Lane,
London W12 0TT

© Text selection by Sara Strange

ISBN: 0 563 34351 6

Set in 12 on 14pt Century Schoolbook by
Keyspools Limited, Warrington

Printed and bound in Great Britain by
Ebenezer Baylis & Son Ltd,
The Trinity Press,
Worcester, and London

foreword

Wind up the clock
What does it say?
It's time to play
PLAYTIME

Playtime has been a popular BBC School Radio series for many years and the invitation to wind up the clock signals to countless children listening at home with a parent, or at nursery or their playgroup, that it's time to sing and dance before settling down to enjoy a good story together.

    This multi-purpose book reflects that sharing atmosphere with a selection of beautifully illustrated stories and poems gathered from the most requested material from the programmes. The wide range of simple and attractive activities will stimulate hours of creative and enjoyable play all year round, making this the perfect companion for the under fives.

contents

continued overleaf

hello, hello

Hello, hello

'Hello, hello, hello, sir
Meet me at the grocer.'
'No, sir,'
'Why, sir?'
'Because I have a cold, sir.'
'Where did you get your cold, sir?'
'At the North Pole, sir.'
'What were you doing there, sir?'
'Visiting polar bears, sir.'
'Let me hear you sneeze, sir.'
'Atchoo! Atchoo! Atchoo!'

Traditional

Hello, goodbye

'Hello, hello,
How do you do?'
You say 'Hello' to me
And I say 'Hello' to you
Now here's a funny thing
So you can tell me why
We often say 'Hello' (Hello!)
And then we say 'Goodbye'.

Chris Warde

Soolee and the white butterfly
by Patricia Taylor

Soolee was four years old. She often looked quiet and shy, but when she smiled her face would break into a big cheeky grin. She wasn't smiling now though. Today she had to start school and she was very cross about it. On the way she grumbled to her Dad.

'Who can I talk to?' she stormed. 'You know I won't like the dinners. Why can't I stay at home like Deedee?'

'You'll like it when you get there,' Dad said.

'I won't. You always say that,' said Soolee.

Dad and Soolee arrived at school and went into the classroom. 'Oh no,' groaned Soolee. '*All* those children.' She hid under her Dad's jacket.

Soolee wasn't just frightened. She felt angry too. She just couldn't understand why she had to start school and her small brother didn't. At home in Japan, where Soolee came from, she had lots of friends, but here no one could understand her and she felt very lonely.

Dad pulled her from under his jacket and said he could stay at school with her for the morning. Soolee sighed with relief.

A girl came to show her where to put her coat. 'Say hello to Nisha,' said Dad. Soolee had practised saying hello and she whispered it very quietly, thinking how silly it all sounded.

On the table were some pencils, paper and scissors. Normally Soolee loved to make things, but she felt so miserable that she just wanted to go home.

The window was open and suddenly the children started to shout and point. A white butterfly had flown through the window and landed on the table near Soolee. Soolee forgot to be angry and she gently caught the butterfly in her hands. Without hurting it, she took it to the window and let it fly free. The children clapped their hands. Soolee looked surprised and then she went back to her table with a big cheeky grin.

She took the paper and began to fold it. Then she used the scissors and when she opened the paper she had made a beautiful white butterfly. 'Look, a butterfly,' the children cried. 'Can we make one?'

Soolee grinned and picked up another piece of paper and began to fold it carefully. She hardly noticed her Dad kissing her goodbye, she was much too busy showing her new friends how to make their beautiful butterflies. 'You don't need to speak the same language when you really want to make friends,' thought Soolee.

Activities for groups of children

o   Play blindfold games
Use a thick scarf to blindfold a child who would like to take part
in the game. Point to another child to come and stand in front of
them. Ask the first child to use their fingers to touch their
partner's face and to describe what they can feel, e.g. long hair,
curly hair, smooth skin, glasses, earrings and so on. Can the
blindfolded child guess who their partner is?

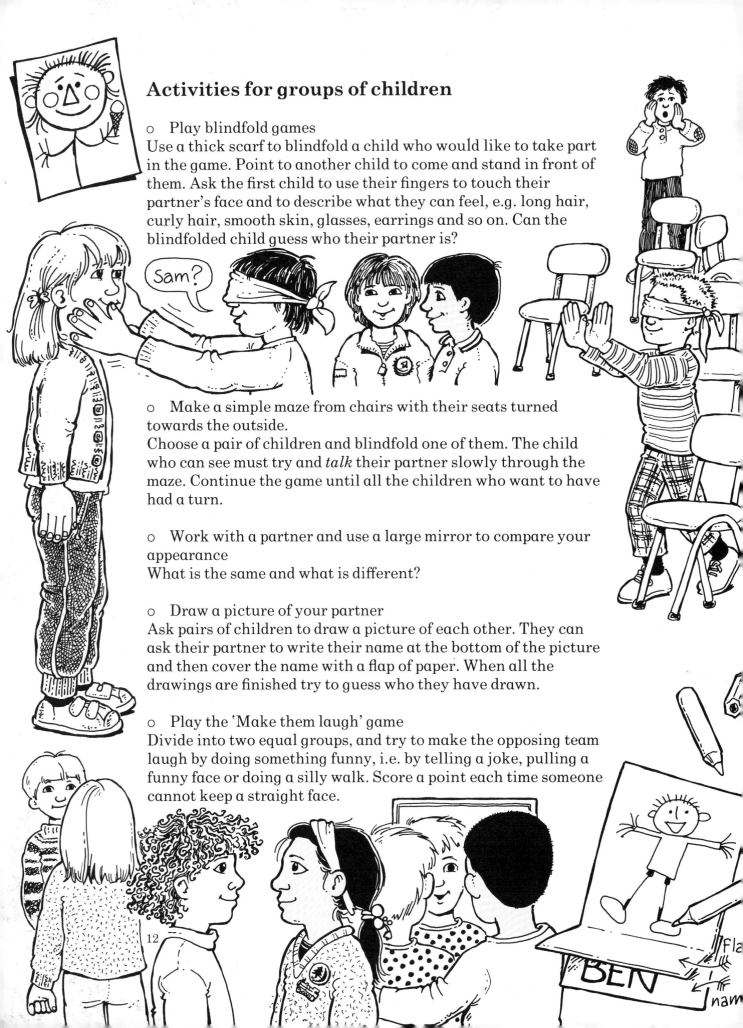

Sam?

o   Make a simple maze from chairs with their seats turned
towards the outside.
Choose a pair of children and blindfold one of them. The child
who can see must try and *talk* their partner slowly through the
maze. Continue the game until all the children who want to have
had a turn.

o   Work with a partner and use a large mirror to compare your
appearance
What is the same and what is different?

o   Draw a picture of your partner
Ask pairs of children to draw a picture of each other. They can
ask their partner to write their name at the bottom of the picture
and then cover the name with a flap of paper. When all the
drawings are finished try to guess who they have drawn.

o   Play the 'Make them laugh' game
Divide into two equal groups, and try to make the opposing team
laugh by doing something funny, i.e. by telling a joke, pulling a
funny face or doing a silly walk. Score a point each time someone
cannot keep a straight face.

BEN

nam

12

Follow-up activities

o   Make a butterfly like Soolee. Place two circular objects, one larger than the other, on a sheet of folded paper and draw round them. Leave a triangle for the butterfly's body. Cut out the shape and then open it up. Attach a pipe-cleaner to make the butterfly's antennae and decorate the wings with paint, sticky paper, glitter or shiny material.

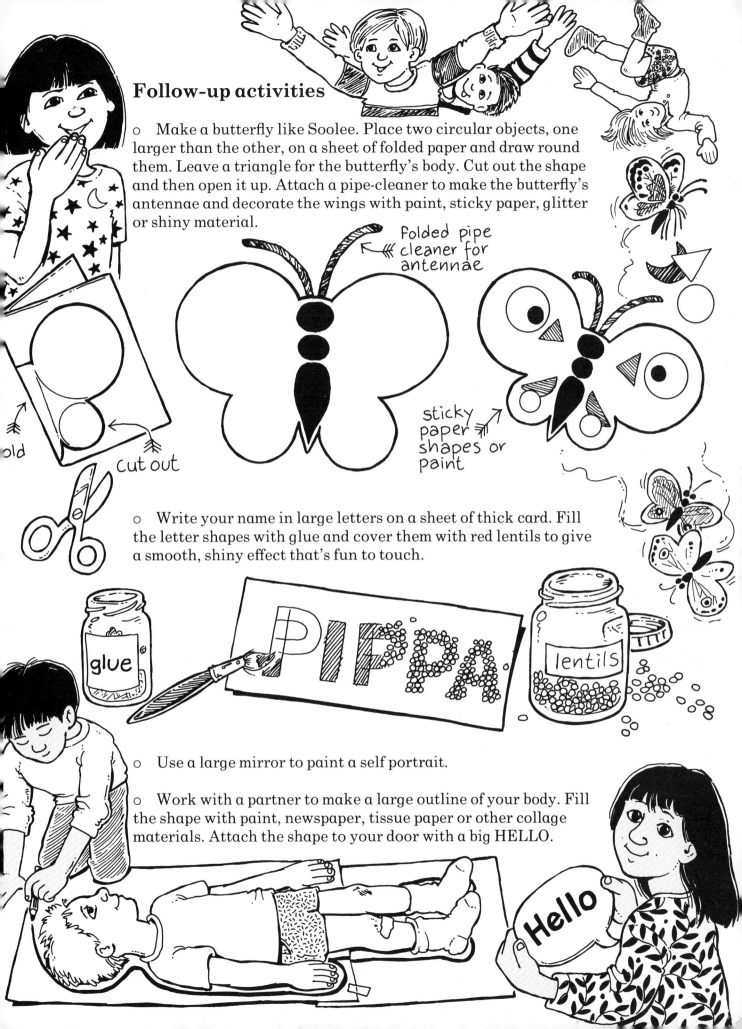

folded pipe cleaner for antennae

fold

cut out

sticky paper shapes or paint

o   Write your name in large letters on a sheet of thick card. Fill the letter shapes with glue and cover them with red lentils to give a smooth, shiny effect that's fun to touch.

glue

PIPPA

lentils

o   Use a large mirror to paint a self portrait.

o   Work with a partner to make a large outline of your body. Fill the shape with paint, newspaper, tissue paper or other collage materials. Attach the shape to your door with a big HELLO.

Hello

this is me

How do you feel?

Ronald Zachary Taylor

Jauntily

1 When the snow is fall - ing not for ve - ry long,

Come out in the snow - flakes and catch them on your

Chorus

tongue! *It makes me hap - py, it makes me smile,*

It makes me hap - py, it makes me smile.

After it's been raining on my way to school,
I will put on wellies and splash in ev'ry pool!

Chorus

Floating things in water, conkers on a string,
Listening to stories, and playing on a swing!

Chorus

Crawling thro' a tunnel, racing with a chum,
Playing with a kitten, and banging on a drum!

Chorus

Great Aunt Nina
by Nora Windridge

Great Aunt Nina was old, very old indeed. 'I can't knit *clever* things any more,' she said when Roger told her about the new baby. 'I can only knit easy things with my old fingers. When you were born I made you a shawl,' she recalled. 'Lacy and white with patterns of flowers and birds and leaves. But I can't make lacy shawls nowadays. My fingers are crooked and old.'

'Everyone makes something,' Roger said. 'I'm making a woolly ball to hang by the pram.'

Great Aunt Nina smiled. 'I'll make the baby a Storytime Blanket,' she told him. 'I can do *that*. The wool is in that bag by my chair. Red, green, yellow, pink, white and blue . . .'

'. . . and brown and orange and purple,' Roger said peeping at the woolly balls in the knitting bag. Great Aunt Nina agreed. 'Even my old fingers can knit the wool into squares and sew them into a Storytime Blanket for your new baby.'

'But where are the stories?' Roger asked. 'Why do you call it a Storytime Blanket, Great Aunt Nina?'

'Every ball of wool is a story to me,' the old lady told Roger. 'Every ball of wool is left over from something else that I've made. That blue ball there is left over from a sweater that I made your big cousin Tom the year that he went to France. And the speckledy-green is the cardigan that Aunt Margaret wears when she digs in the garden – it was her best cardigan once.'

'And the khaki-brown?

'*That* made socks for soldiers long ago,' Great Aunt Nina said.

'And this purple square?' Roger said, carefully picking out the woolly squares from Great Aunt Nina's bag.

'*That's* over from Mummy's thick jersey that she wears when the wind is cold! When I have knitted enough I shall sew the squares together into a fine blanket. Every square tells a story to me. As I knit along, stitch along, purl and plain, I tell myself stories about Cousin Tom and Auntie Margaret, and the rest of the family. That white ball of wool is *especially* special. That's over from the very last lacy shawl that I made. The shawl that I made for *you*, Roger, when you were the baby on the way.'

'Could I knit a square?' Roger asked. 'A square for your Storytime Blanket, Aunt Nina?'

'If you learn to knit,' she said. 'If my old fingers can teach you.'

'Let me try,' Roger said. 'And when all the squares are knitted and sewn together, what a lovely blanket we'll have – a Storytime Blanket to wrap round our baby. That's as nice as a woolly white shawl any day. *That's* what I think, Great Aunt Nina!'

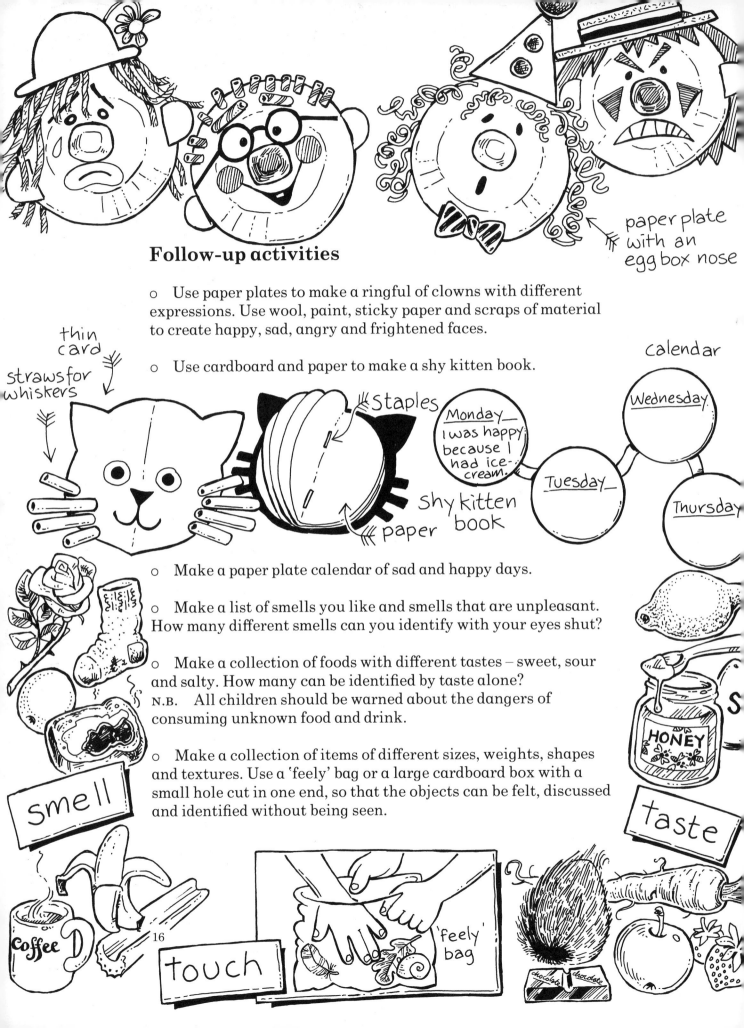

paper plate
with an
egg box nose

Follow-up activities

o Use paper plates to make a ringful of clowns with different expressions. Use wool, paint, sticky paper and scraps of material to create happy, sad, angry and frightened faces.

o Use cardboard and paper to make a shy kitten book.

thin card

straws for whiskers

Staples

paper

shy kitten book

calendar

Monday_ I was happy because I had ice-cream.

Tuesday_

Wednesday

Thursday

o Make a paper plate calendar of sad and happy days.

o Make a list of smells you like and smells that are unpleasant. How many different smells can you identify with your eyes shut?

o Make a collection of foods with different tastes – sweet, sour and salty. How many can be identified by taste alone?
N.B. All children should be warned about the dangers of consuming unknown food and drink.

o Make a collection of items of different sizes, weights, shapes and textures. Use a 'feely' bag or a large cardboard box with a small hole cut in one end, so that the objects can be felt, discussed and identified without being seen.

smell

taste

HONEY

coffee

touch

'feely' bag

fox

fish

shells

o X-rays of bones and teeth are a wonderful insight into our bodies. Skulls and skeletons from animals and birds make interesting comparisons.

o Bones and muscles help us move. Hold the top of your arm and feel what happens when you bend and straighten your elbow.

parrot

frog

duck

rabbit

leg bone

o Muscles can only shorten or contract. They always pull, they cannot push. Pull some funny faces and try to feel the muscles in your face.

o Explore the different ways your body can move and discover where some of the joints are. Make a model skeleton from pieces of card joined with paper clips to show where the major joints are.

paper fasteners

skeleton

stretch person

o Make fingerprint pictures.

o Make a stretch person.

fold

cut on the lines

add arms head and feet.

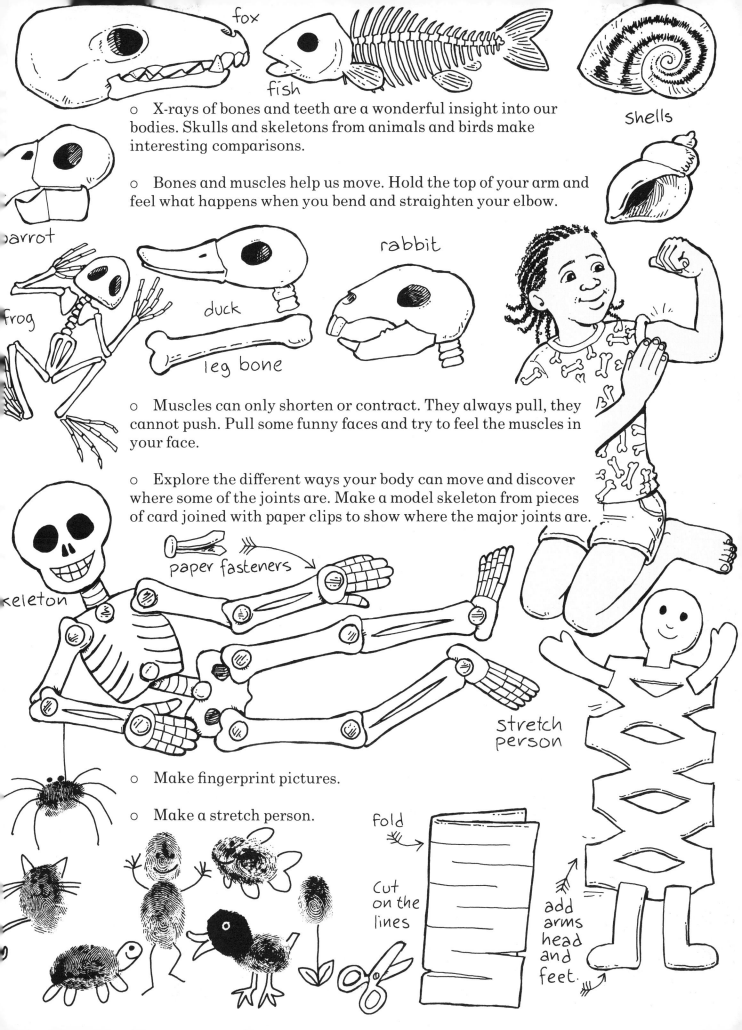

my house

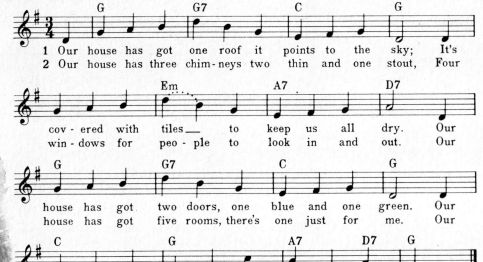

Our house

Ronald Zachary Taylor

1 Our house has got one roof it points to the sky; It's
2 Our house has three chim-neys two thin and one stout, Four

cov-ered with tiles___ to keep us all dry. Our
win-dows for peo-ple to look in and out. Our

house has got two doors, one blue and one green. Our
house has got five rooms, there's one just for me. Our

house is the pret-tiest that you've ev-er seen.
house is our home, won't you come round for tea?

Joanne moves house
by Hazel Glynn

'I won't go!' shouted Joanne.

'What do you mean you won't go?' asked Mum.

I'm not moving to a new flat, I like it here!' replied Joanne.

'Wait 'till you see it. You'll change your mind,' said Dad.

'I won't,' said Joanne.

'It's got a huge playground and garden next to the block,' continued Dad.

'I don't care,' said Joanne, 'My friends won't be there!'

'You'll make new friends,' persisted Mum.

'Not like Imran!' said Joanne, and she ran out of the room.

She had an idea. She'd ask Imran's Mum if she could live with them. After all, they did have a spare bed. She'd go straight away. She walked down the corridor to Flat 92 and knocked on the door.

'Hello, Mrs Khan,' she said. 'Mum and Dad are moving, so can I come and live with you and Imran?'

'Well,' said Mrs Khan, 'I don't think it would be a good idea to leave your Mum and Dad just yet. After all, you're only five aren't you?'

'Yes, but I don't want to move to a new flat!' continued Joanne.

'I tell you what,' said Mrs Khan, 'You can stay here whenever you want and Imran will be able to visit you.'

Joanne returned home. Her plan hadn't worked. If she couldn't live with Imran, then she supposed she'd have to move house with Mum and Dad.

The next week kept them all very busy. Joanne packed her toys into large boxes. Cupboards and wardrobes were emptied and Mum and Dad spent hours carefully putting everything into tea chests. The flat looked strange with piles of plates, books and clothes all over the place.

Finally moving day arrived. Mum, Dad and Joanne took a last look at the flat. It looked very different without any pictures on the walls or furniture in the rooms. 'Goodbye Flat,' said Joanne as she walked to each room in turn. Mum and Dad were quiet as they closed the door behind them for the last time.

'I still don't want to go,' said Joanne.

'We know that,' said Dad, 'We also feel sad in a way, but I'm sure you'll get to like the new flat in time.'

When they arrrived at the flat, the first thing Joanne noticed were the swings and slide next to the block. There was even a climbing frame. 'But what's the use if I've got to play on my own,' she thought.

When all the furniture had been carried into the new flat, Mum, Dad and Joanne sat down amongst the tea chests and drank tea from paper cups. Then there was a knock at the door. 'Who can that be?' said Mum as she went to answer it. She came back in followed by a woman and a boy who looked about four years old.

'We've come to welcome you to the block,' said Sue Jones. 'It'll be nice for Sean to have someone to play with again. He's been quite lonely since his best friend Natasha moved away.'

Sean turned to Joanne. 'Would you like to have a go on the climbing frame?'

Joanne thought that sounded like a good idea. 'It looks as if I'm not the only one to miss people when they move,' she said as she followed Sean out into the playground. 'Perhaps the new flat won't be so bad after all!'

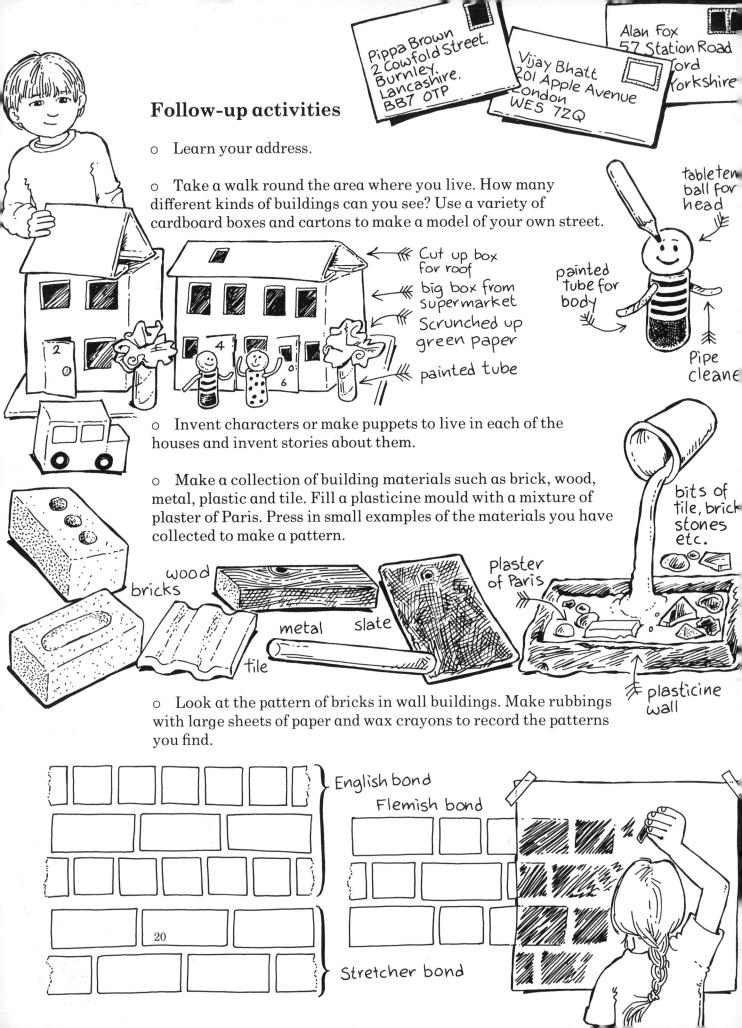

Follow-up activities

o   Learn your address.

o   Take a walk round the area where you live. How many different kinds of buildings can you see? Use a variety of cardboard boxes and cartons to make a model of your own street.

Cut up box for roof

big box from supermarket

Scrunched up green paper

painted tube

tabletennis ball for head

painted tube for body

Pipe cleaner

o   Invent characters or make puppets to live in each of the houses and invent stories about them.

o   Make a collection of building materials such as brick, wood, metal, plastic and tile. Fill a plasticine mould with a mixture of plaster of Paris. Press in small examples of the materials you have collected to make a pattern.

bricks

wood

metal

tile

slate

Plaster of Paris

bits of tile, brick stones etc.

plasticine wall

o   Look at the pattern of bricks in wall buildings. Make rubbings with large sheets of paper and wax crayons to record the patterns you find.

English bond

Flemish bond

Stretcher bond

20

Pippa Brown
2 Cowfold Street,
Burnley,
Lancashire.
BB7 OTP

Vijay Bhatt
201 Apple Avenue
London
WE5 7ZQ

Alan Fox
57 Station Road
ford
Yorkshire

triangles

squares

hexagons

o   Experiment with shapes cut from sticky paper to find out if there are any other shapes that fit together like bricks. How many different patterns can you make?

o   Act out the story of the *Three Little Pigs*.

masks of card or thick paper

paper cup nose

pigs

straw

sticks

bricks

Wolf

stuffed sock tail

o   Use large cardboard boxes, newspaper, old blankets, long canes, string and so on to make a shelter.

o   Animals, birds, fish and insects make homes in the most surprising places. How many examples can you find?

Woodpecker

wasps

hermit crab

beaver

my street

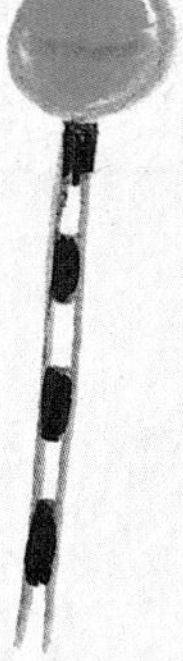

Red for danger

In the busy bustling town,
Traffic rushing up and down.

People in a hurry,
People in a scurry –
Got to shop, mustn't stop,
Friends to meet, cross the street –
Mrs Jones, hello, can't stop,
Got to get to the baker's shop,
Here's the crossing – light is red –
Must get across to buy my bread.

That car's not coming very fast,
If we are quick we can get past. . . .'

'MUMMY, MUMMY, haven't you seen –
You mustn't cross 'till the light is GREEN –
That light is RED and RED spells DANGER.'

'I'm sorry son, of course you're right –
We must take notice of the light.'

Angela Garner

Litter

Litter in the playground, litter in the street,
Litter at the bus stop, litter at your feet;
Litter in the pictures, litter at the fair,
Litter, litter, litter, litter, litter everywhere.

If every piece of litter was worth its weight in gold,
There wouldn't be a single piece of litter to behold;
It isn't worth a penny but it's worth a little care,
To keep the place much cleaner, much cleaner everywhere.

Roland Egon

22

The five houses
by Janet Sorensen

There were five little houses in the row, each with a front door in the front . . . of course! And each with a garden, and a back gate, at the back . . . of course! By each back gate was a dustbin and in each garden was a washing line. But there were not five cars in the five garages at the end of the lane.

The man at number 2 had a smart, brown car. The lady at number 3 had a little blue car that went in 'fits and starts'. The lady in number 5 had a white 'jallopy' that was broken. Mrs 4 . . . only had a wheelbarrow . . . and Mrs 1 . . . just had a shopping trolley.

Every morning at different times they came down to put rubbish in their dustbin (Miss 3 had a new rubber bin). But they never met each other.

On Monday Mrs 1 washed her pink sheets and blue pyjamas; on Tuesday Mr 2 washed his stripey jersey and gardening socks; on Wednesday Miss 3 washed her red jersey and grey towels; on Thursday Mrs 4 washed her spotty apron and tea towels, and on Friday Miss 5 washed a lot of things!. . . . And so they never met!

Mr 2 went to town in his big, brown car; Miss 5 went shopping in her white jallopy; Miss 3 cycled to the farm for her eggs; Mrs 4 walked, and Mrs 1 took her trolley – and somehow they never met!

There were potatoes growing in number 1, flowers in number 2, an apple tree at 3, Mrs 4 had a beautiful lawn and Miss 5 had a huge sunflower.

One sunny morning, Miss 3 thought Tuesday was Wednesday and did her washing; Mrs 4 didn't hear her clock strike; Mrs 1 overslept and got up late, and one by one they began to come down their garden paths at the *same* time!

'Well, well,' said Miss 3 to Mrs 4. . . . 'Well, well, well,' said 1 to 2 and 5. . . . 'Well I never?' And they all began chattering away.

'Let's have a party,' said Miss 3. . . . 'Now that's an idea,' said Mrs 4. . . . 'Why not?' the all said together.

That night by the light of the moon and Mr 2's car lights they had their party on Mrs 4's lovely green lawn.

Mrs 1 made chips from the potatoes in her garden; Mr 2 danced in his stripey jersey; Miss 3 tapped the rhythm on her dustbin lid; Miss 5 rang her bicycle bell. What a time they had!

Of course, they don't have a party every day, or every week – but Mr 2 sometimes takes them shopping in his car; Mrs 1 gives them potatoes for their dinner; Miss 5 has given them all sunflower seeds . . . and they always wave to each other as they go up and down their garden path.

23

Follow-up activities

o   Zebra crossings, pelican crossings and footbridges are all safe places to cross the road. Practise crossing the road safely with an adult to help you.

o   Take a walk down your street. How many different vehicles can you spot? How many can you find with two wheels, three wheels, four wheels and more than four wheels? What jobs do the vehicles do?

o   Hold your own traffic census. Make a tally chart of the different vehicles that pass the spot where you are standing.
Use your tally chart to help you record the results of your census as a picture.

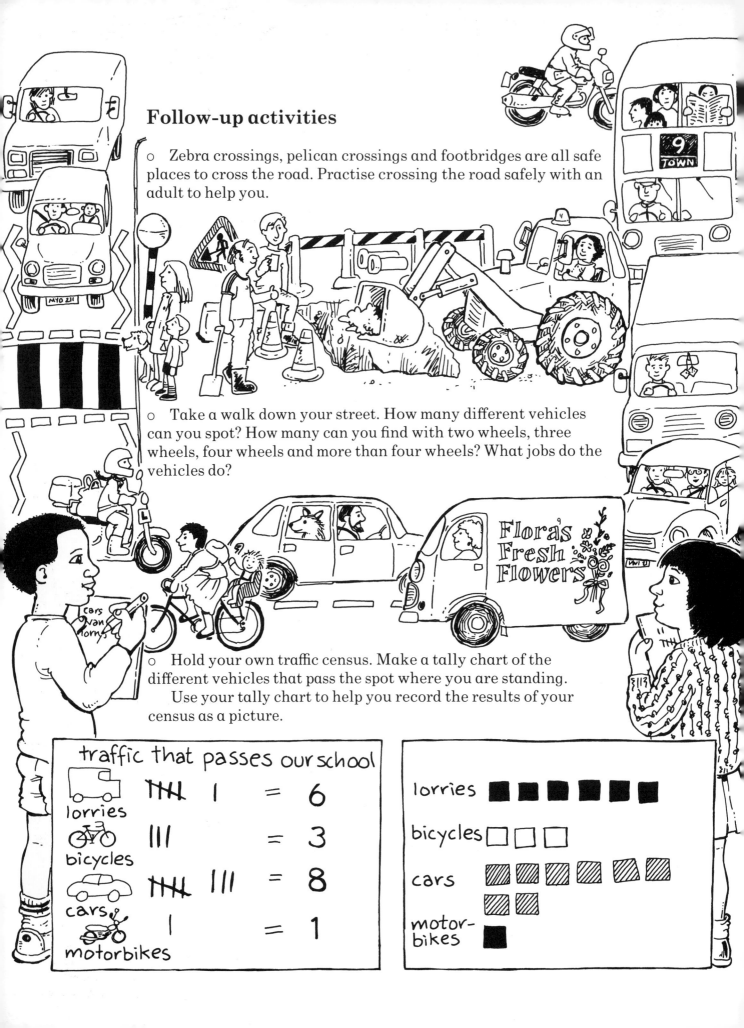

traffic that passes our school

lorries	~~IIII~~ I	=	6
bicycles	III	=	3
cars	~~IIII~~ III	=	8
motorbikes	I	=	1

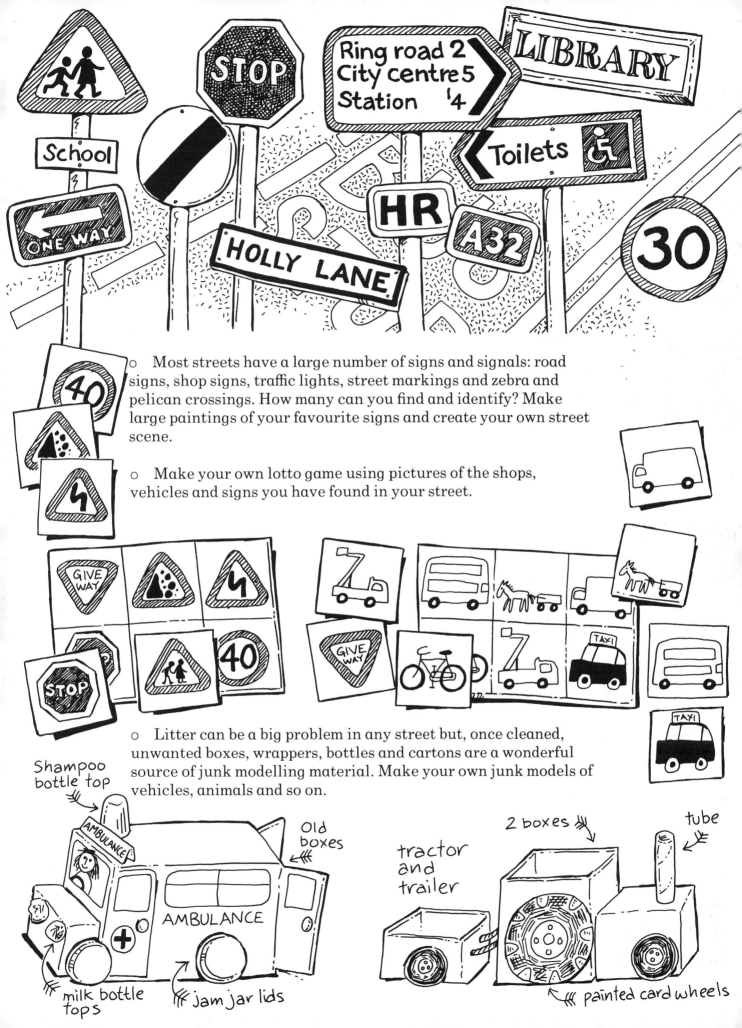

o   Most streets have a large number of signs and signals: road signs, shop signs, traffic lights, street markings and zebra and pelican crossings. How many can you find and identify? Make large paintings of your favourite signs and create your own street scene.

o   Make your own lotto game using pictures of the shops, vehicles and signs you have found in your street.

o   Litter can be a big problem in any street but, once cleaned, unwanted boxes, wrappers, bottles and cartons are a wonderful source of junk modelling material. Make your own junk models of vehicles, animals and so on.

Shampoo bottle top

Old boxes

AMBULANCE

milk bottle tops

jam jar lids

tractor and trailer

2 boxes

tube

painted card wheels

starting school

Don't be late

Ronald Zachary Taylor

1 Ev-'ry week-day morn-ing ear-ly I go out to meet my
chums If its rain or shine whe-ther wet or fine We all
say bye-bye to mums. *Chorus* It's a spe-cial place we go to where we
have a gold-en rule *Don't be late!* (clap clap) *Don't be
late!* (clap clap) *Don't be late, don't be late for school!*

In our lessons we learn numbers,
How to add and take away,
How to read and write, how to fly a kite
First we work and then we play.

Repeat chorus

No time for elephants
by Angela Pickering

'I'm going to Nursery School today,' said Mary Lou. 'There's such a lot to do. No time for breakfast. No *thank you*!'
'Oh,' said Mary Lou's Mummy. 'Not even a nice boiled egg?' Mary Lou's Mummy put a boiled egg on the table. It was brown and speckly and as warm as the sun.
'Well,' said Mary Lou, looking at the egg. 'I'll just have a nibble. I might get hungry at Nursery School.'

26

So Mary Lou ate her boiled egg. Then she cleaned her teeth and brushed her hair and washed her face and kissed both her teddies goodbye – the big teddy with the squeak and the little teddy with no hair. Now she was ready for Nursery School.

'What about your coat?' said Mummy.

'But I'm going to Nursery School today!' said Mary Lou. 'There's such a lot to do. I stopped to eat my boiled egg. I cleaned my teeth and brushed my hair and washed my face. I kissed both my teddies goodbye – the big teddy with the squeak and the little teddy with no hair. No time for coats. No *thank you*.'

'Not even your new blue coat with the furry lining?' said Mummy.

Mary Lou looked at the coat. It was soft and blue and the furry lining was so cosy. It was like the inside of a nest. 'Well, perhaps I will just slip it on,' said Mary Lou. 'It might be cold at Nursery.'

So Mary Lou and her Mummy were ready for Nursery School. They opened the door and there stood the postman. 'Hello, young lady,' said the postman. 'I've got a postcard for you.'

'But I'm going to Nursery School today!' said Mary Lou. 'There's such a lot to do. I stopped to eat my boiled egg. I cleaned my teeth and brushed my hair and washed my face. I kissed both my teddies goodbye – the big teddy with the squeak and the little teddy with no hair. And I put on my coat with the new blue lining. No time for postcards. No *thank you*.'

'Not even for a postcard from the seaside?' said the postman.

Mary Lou looked at the postcard. It was from her Granny. It showed some donkeys on the sand, and the big blue sea in the distance. 'Well, perhaps I'll pop it in my pocket,' said Mary Lou.

Then off they went, Mary Lou and her Mummy, off to Nursery.

At the corner of the street, Mary Lou met an *elephant*. A huge grey elephant marching to the zoo. 'Come and see,' called a man. 'Come and see the elephant feeding at the zoo.'

'Oh dear,' said Mary Lou. 'But I'm going to *Nursery School* today! There's such a lot to do. I stopped to eat my boiled egg. I cleaned my teeth and brushed my hair and washed my face. I kissed both my teddies goodbye – the big teddy with the squeak and the little teddy with no hair. I put on my coat with the new blue lining and the postman came with a card from the seaside. No time for elephants. No *thank you*.' And she burst into tears.

'There, there,' said the man. 'I don't mean this very minute. We feed the elephants every day at the zoo. Come along on Sunday, when you're not going to Nursery School.' Then the man smiled, and Mary Lou's Mummy smiled, and Mary Lou smiled and the elephant waved its trunk in the air and looked quite happy too.

As for Mary Lou, on she went to Nursery School and she was just in time!

$2+2=$ $1+4=$ $2+3=$ $1+3=$

Monday	Tuesday	Wednesday	Thursday	Friday	Saturday	Sunday
~~14~~	~~13~~	12	11	10	9	8
7	6	5	4	3	2	1
School starts					No school	

STOP CHILDREN

Follow-up activities

o Make a simple calendar, showing the days until school starts. Colour in one square each day.

o Arrange a visit to your local school to meet some of the people who work there: the head teacher, class teachers, caretaker, cooks and meal supervisors. Find out what jobs they do and, if possible, watch them at work.

Back at home, dress up in old clothes and hats and act out some of the jobs.

Spring
Summer
Autumn
Winter

o Use dolls and teddies to set up your own school at home.

o Use chalk to draw your own school pictures.

o Talk to grandparents or older people about their experiences of school long ago. Ask them to describe the clothes they wore, the lessons they studied and the games they played.

o Make a picture timetable showing the order of activities in class each day.

Monday	$1+5=6$ sums	milk	playtime	painting	lunch	story
Tuesday	abcd writing	milk	playtime	games	lunch	story
Wednesday	$2+3=5$ sums	milk	playtime	nature table	lunch	

o   Find out more about the history of your school. Plant a tree to mark your school's birthday.

o   Cut three different lengths of string – 25 cm, 50 cm and 100 cm. Arrange the strings in order according to their length. Thread a bead on to each length of string. Knot the ends of the string together and, making sure the bead is in the centre, suspend the loop from a length of cane, balanced between two chairs. Repeat this with the other two pieces of string. What will happen when you push the beads and make them swing? Is there a relationship between the length of the string and the speed of the swing?

o   Make a simple see-saw from a ruler and a cotton reel. Make sure the ruler is balanced. Where does the cotton reel have to be? Place a weight at one end of the ruler. Can the see-saw be balanced again? What happens if the weight is moved forward on the see-saw?

o   The playground is a safe place to play. Make a zig-zag book about other safe places to play.

o   Play hopscotch.

o   **Holly the Hedgehog**   *Patricia Taylor*

Holly the Hedgehog couldn't keep still.
Holly the Hedgehog went up the hill.
'Oh,' said Holly, 'Come with me,
I can see things that begin with *b*.
I see a ball which bounces high
I see a little bird in the sky
I see a bridge that crosses the stream
I see a boy with a big ice-cream.'

o   Draw a picture about all the things Holly can see, beginning with the letter *b*. Perhaps you can think of some more.
    Make up your own sentences about the things Holly can see beginning with other letters, e.g. 'I can see cats creeping by'.

29

plasticine weight

see-saw

ruler

cotton reel

food

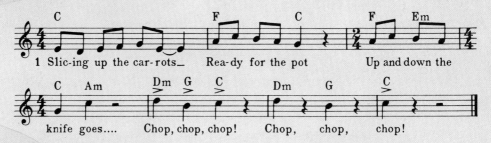

Chop, chop, chop

Jerry O'Regan

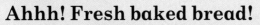

1 Slic-ing up the car-rots__ Rea-dy for the pot Up and down the knife goes.... Chop, chop, chop! Chop, chop, chop!

Scrubbing the potatoes	Round and round the mixing bowl
Cleaning off the mud	Stirring up a batter
To and fro the brush goes	Round and round the spoon goes
Scrub, scrub, scrub.	Clatter, clatter, clatter.

Rolling out the pastry
With the rolling pin
Roll it smooth, roll it flat
Rolling out and in.

Ahhh! Fresh baked bread!
by Ann Burnett

Mr Mathieson was the village baker. Every morning, very early, he would get up and go down to his bakehouse to bake the bread for that day. On Mondays he would make lovely floury, white loaves; on Tuesdays, crusty brown bread; on Wednesdays, great round loaves with little round ones on top, called cottage loaves. He twisted the dough into fancy shapes on Thursdays to make plaited loaves and on Fridays and Saturdays he was very busy baking all sorts of bread and rolls and, if he had time, cakes. On Sundays, he sat out in his garden if it was nice.

Mr Mathieson always knew when his bread was ready by the smell. SNIFF SNIFF SNIIIFFF! he would go. 'No, not quite ready, another five minutes yet,' he'd say. 'SNIFF SNIFF SNIIIFFF! Ah yes,

that's just perfect.' And he'd open up the oven and take out the steaming hot loaves.

'Ahhhh!' the villagers would say, as the smell wafted down the street. 'Mr Mathieson's bread's ready.' And they would put on their coats and take their shopping bags and hurry down to the baker's to buy some of the freshly baked bread.

One morning, instead of the usual smell of baking bread, a strong smell of burning drifted through the village. 'What on earth is Mr Mathieson doing?' said all the villagers. They hurried along to the baker's to see what was wrong.

Mr Mathieson was standing behind his counter looking very glum. Instead of nice floury, crusty loaves, the shelves were filled with black, burnt lumps.

'Oh dear, whatever's happened?' everyone asked him. 'What have you done to the bread?'

'I've dot a bad coad and I can't smell anyding,' moaned Mr Mathieson. 'My dose is all stuffed up.' He went to bed with his hot water bottle and a box of paper handkerchiefs and the villagers were left without any bread.

What on earth were they to do? Mrs Finlayson made scones and put cheese on them for her husband's lunch.

'What's this?' he grumbled. 'Where's the bread?'

'There isn't any,' Mrs Finlayson said. 'Mr Mathieson's got a bad cold.'

Mrs McIvor made potato cakes for her children's lunch. 'Why can't we have bread?' they complained. 'We can't put strawberry jam on potato cakes.'

'Mr Mathieson can't bake bread till he's got rid of his cold,' Mrs McIvor explained.

'Oh dear,' the villagers all said. 'What will we do without any bread? Hurry up and get well, Mr Mathieson!'

Then one morning, Mrs Finlayson jumped out of bed and gave a great big SNIFF. 'Bread!' she exclaimed. 'I smell bread!' And she threw on her clothes, grabbed her shopping bag and purse and dashed up to the baker's.

On the way, she was joined by the rest of the village all sniffing loudly as they went. 'Bread! We smell bread!'

In the baker's, there was Mr Mathieson smiling broadly. 'My cold's all gone and I can smell the bread baking. SNIFF SNIFF SNIIIFFF! Yes, it's just ready.' And he opened the oven and took out the crusty hot loaves. 'Ahhhh!' sniffed the villagers. 'Fresh baked bread!'

Kiwi Fruit

runner beans

broad beans

Follow-up activities

o   Visit the market and make a collection of fruit and vegetables to taste. Include some more unusual fruit in your purchases, e.g. a kiwi fruit, a mango, an ugli fruit, a pomegranate. Sort the fruits and vegetables by their shapes, colours and sizes.

o   Make fruit and vegetable prints.

saucers of paint

Carrot
apple
potato

bean sprou

Pomegranate

o   Make individual fruit pies. Weigh, mix and roll the ingredients for the pastry and add a variety of prepared fruit, according to the season.

apple card

o   Make apple cards.

o   Plan and draw a menu for a day.

fold

Today's Menu

Breakfast
Cornflakes
Boiled egg
milk
lunch
stew
potato
peas
apple pie

Tea
toast
honey
yoghurt
orange

supper
cocoa
biscuit

24 wheaty Bricks

24 wheaty Bricks

Flour

o   Collect wrappers, labels and pictures of food, and sort them into different groups: fats, e.g. butter, cheese; carbohydrates, e.g. biscuits, bread, potatoes; protein, e.g. fish, meat, eggs, cheese; fruit; vegetables.

o   Grow mustard and cress, and make your own sandwiches to take on a picnic.

cress

chocolate Biscuits

RICE PUDDING RA

BREAD
BROWN HARVESTGRAIN
SLICED

MARGARINE
Sunflower
MARGARINE

Spaghetti

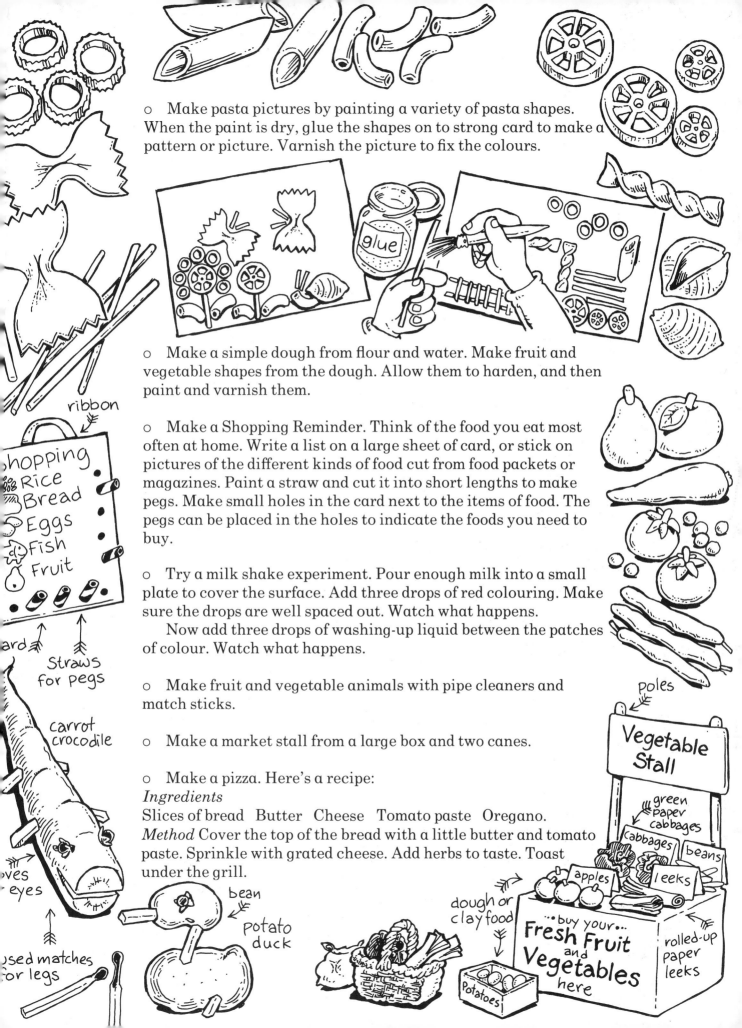

o   Make pasta pictures by painting a variety of pasta shapes. When the paint is dry, glue the shapes on to strong card to make a pattern or picture. Varnish the picture to fix the colours.

glue

o   Make a simple dough from flour and water. Make fruit and vegetable shapes from the dough. Allow them to harden, and then paint and varnish them.

o   Make a Shopping Reminder. Think of the food you eat most often at home. Write a list on a large sheet of card, or stick on pictures of the different kinds of food cut from food packets or magazines. Paint a straw and cut it into short lengths to make pegs. Make small holes in the card next to the items of food. The pegs can be placed in the holes to indicate the foods you need to buy.

o   Try a milk shake experiment. Pour enough milk into a small plate to cover the surface. Add three drops of red colouring. Make sure the drops are well spaced out. Watch what happens.
    Now add three drops of washing-up liquid between the patches of colour. Watch what happens.

o   Make fruit and vegetable animals with pipe cleaners and match sticks.

o   Make a market stall from a large box and two canes.

o   Make a pizza. Here's a recipe:
Ingredients
Slices of bread Butter Cheese Tomato paste Oregano.
Method Cover the top of the bread with a little butter and tomato paste. Sprinkle with grated cheese. Add herbs to taste. Toast under the grill.

ribbon

Shopping
Rice
Bread
Eggs
Fish
Fruit

card

Straws
for pegs

carrot
crocodile

ves
eyes

used matches
for legs

bean

potato
duck

poles

Vegetable
Stall

green
paper
cabbages

cabbages

beans

apples

leeks

dough or
clay food

..buy your..
Fresh Fruit
and
Vegetables
here

Potatoes

rolled-up
paper
leeks

clothes

Choosing shoes

New shoes, new shoes,
Red and pink and blue shoes,
Tell me what would *you* choose
If they'd let us buy?

Buckle shoes, bow shoes,
Pretty pointy-toe shoes,
Strappy, cappy low shoes;
Let's have some to try.

Bright shoes, white shoes,
Dandy dance-by-night shoes,
Perhaps-a-little-tight shoes;
Like some? So would I.

BUT
Flat shoes, fat shoes
Stump-along-like-that shoes,
Wipe-them-on-the-mat shoes
O that's the sort they'll buy.

Frida Wolfe

John

John could take his clothes off
but could not put them on.
His patient mother dressed him,
and said to little John,
'Now, John!
You keep your things on.'

But John had long since gone –
and left a trail of sneakers
and small things in the sun,
so she would know to find him
wherever he might run.

And at the end of every trail
stood Mrs Jones & Son,
she with all his little clothes,
and little John – with none!

For John could take his clothes off
but could not put them on.
His patient mother dressed him
and on went little John –
and on –
    and on –
        and on –

N M Bodecker

New Clothes and Old

I rather like New Clothes,
They make me feel so fine,
Yet I am not quite Me,
The Clothes are not quite mine,

I really love Old Clothes,
The make me feel so free,
I know that they are mine,
For I feel just like Me.

Eleanor Farjeon

Dragon looks for a coat
By Joy Gammon

Once upon a time, Dragon was walking through his wood, when he realised that it was beginning to be very cold. Winter was coming. He needed a coat and decided to ask his friends if he could borrow one from them.

First, he asked Spider. 'May I borrow your hairy coat, please?'

'No, Dragon,' said Spider. 'It is too small and it has too many sleeves for you, but if you watch I will teach you how to spin silver threads like I do.' And he did.

Then Dragon asked Caterpillar. 'May I borrow your beautiful speckled skin, please?'

'No, Dragon' said Caterpillar. 'I still need it myself, but if you watch I will teach you how to weave silk threads together like I do.' And he did.

Next, Dragon asked Hedgehog. 'May I borrow your spikey suit of armour, please?'

'No, Dragon,' said Hedgehog. 'I use it to keep myself safe, but I will give you one of my spines for a needle.' And he did.

Now Dragon asked Hare. 'May I borrow your soft coat, please?'

'No, Dragon,' said Hare. 'Without it I would freeze in the winter, but I will give you some button mushrooms from my field for your coat.' And he did.

Then Dragon asked Sheep. 'May I have some of your curly white wool, please?'

'Yes, of course, Dragon,' said Sheep. 'You may take as much as you like, I will soon grow some more.' And he did.

With the wool, Dragon spun threads as Spider had taught him, wove them into cloth as he had seen Caterpillar do, and used Hedgehog's needle to sew the pieces together into a beautiful white coat. Then he stitched Hare's buttons down the front and put the coat on. Dragon invited all his friends to tea and thanked them for their help, and he wore the beautiful coat every day until the warm spring weather came again.

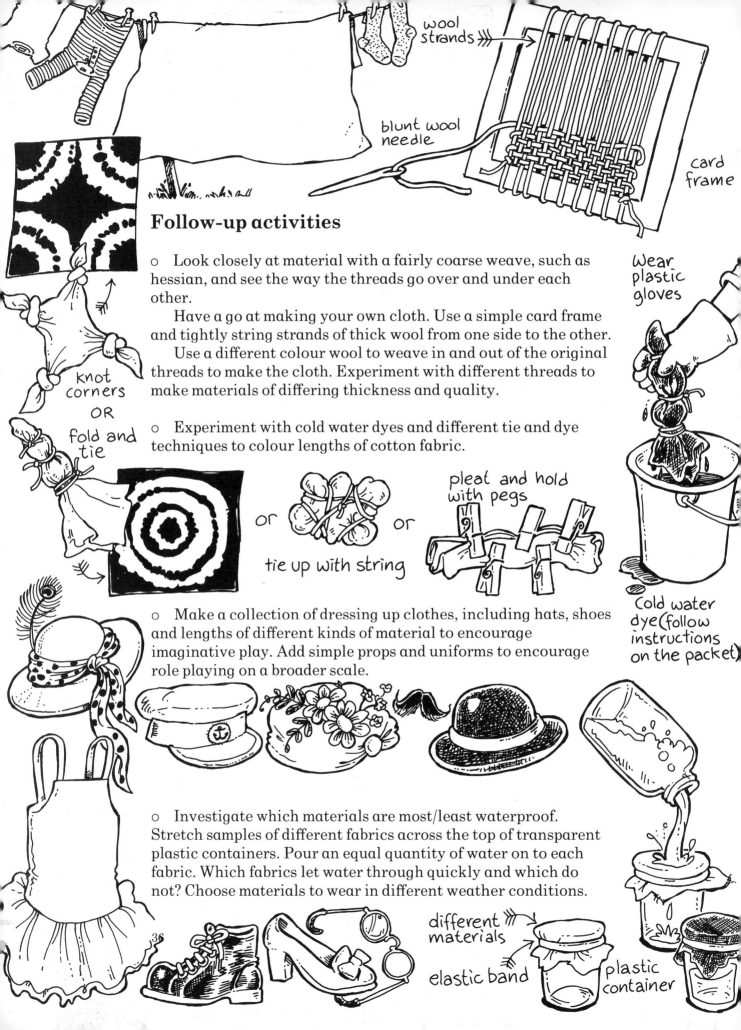

Follow-up activities

o Look closely at material with a fairly coarse weave, such as hessian, and see the way the threads go over and under each other.

Have a go at making your own cloth. Use a simple card frame and tightly string strands of thick wool from one side to the other.

Use a different colour wool to weave in and out of the original threads to make the cloth. Experiment with different threads to make materials of differing thickness and quality.

o Experiment with cold water dyes and different tie and dye techniques to colour lengths of cotton fabric.

o Make a collection of dressing up clothes, including hats, shoes and lengths of different kinds of material to encourage imaginative play. Add simple props and uniforms to encourage role playing on a broader scale.

o Investigate which materials are most/least waterproof. Stretch samples of different fabrics across the top of transparent plastic containers. Pour an equal quantity of water on to each fabric. Which fabrics let water through quickly and which do not? Choose materials to wear in different weather conditions.

wool strands

blunt wool needle

card frame

knot corners OR fold and tie

wear plastic gloves

or tie up with string

or pleat and hold with pegs

Cold water dye (follow instructions on the packet)

different materials

elastic band

plastic container

36

o   Make a collection of pictures of clothes from across the world. Look for similarities and differences. Which clothes are most suitable for hot, wet, cold and dry climates?

o   Special clothes are worn for celebrations, for safety, as uniforms and to keep people clean. Collect pictures to make a colourful display of these special clothes and find out more about why they are worn.

o   Fashion is constantly changing. Design your own set of fashionable clothes and use a collage of different materials, pasted on to large cardboard figures, to bring your drawings to life.

Cut out cardboard figure

Paper fans

bottle tops, etc

SCRAP MATERIALS

tools and machines

The do-it-yourself song

Anne English
Music by Alasdair MacNeill

1 Sand-pa-per, screw-dri-ver, chi-sel and screws, Brush-es all siz-es for
me to choose. Pli-ers and plun-gers, bot-tles and tins, Tools all rea-dy for
me to be-gin.

Chorus
Dab-bet-ty, dab-bet-ty, dab, dab, dab. Rap-pet-ty, rap-pet-ty, rap, rap, rap.
Tap-pet-ty, tap-pet-ty, tap, tap, tap. Biff, Bash, Bang!

Scraper and paintbrush, scissors and saws,
All manner of spanners and hinges for doors.
Wrenches and washers of every type
And a whopping big hammer to bang – the pipe.

Chorus

Eric's extra eye
by Margaret Joy

This story is about Eric, who liked looking at things. He liked
using his eyes to look at things very, very closely.

Sometimes, when it was raining, he liked sitting on the window
sill and watching the rain drops slowly rolling down the glass. It
looked as though the drops were having a race to see which could

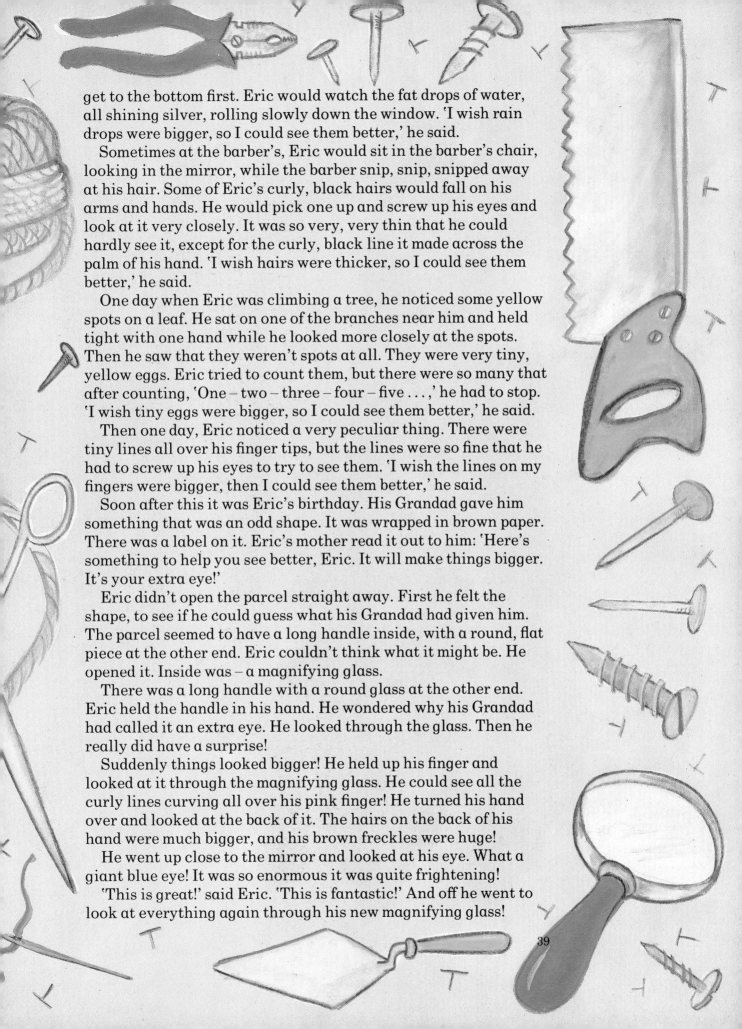

get to the bottom first. Eric would watch the fat drops of water, all shining silver, rolling slowly down the window. 'I wish rain drops were bigger, so I could see them better,' he said.

Sometimes at the barber's, Eric would sit in the barber's chair, looking in the mirror, while the barber snip, snip, snipped away at his hair. Some of Eric's curly, black hairs would fall on his arms and hands. He would pick one up and screw up his eyes and look at it very closely. It was so very, very thin that he could hardly see it, except for the curly, black line it made across the palm of his hand. 'I wish hairs were thicker, so I could see them better,' he said.

One day when Eric was climbing a tree, he noticed some yellow spots on a leaf. He sat on one of the branches near him and held tight with one hand while he looked more closely at the spots. Then he saw that they weren't spots at all. They were very tiny, yellow eggs. Eric tried to count them, but there were so many that after counting, 'One – two – three – four – five . . . ,' he had to stop. 'I wish tiny eggs were bigger, so I could see them better,' he said.

Then one day, Eric noticed a very peculiar thing. There were tiny lines all over his finger tips, but the lines were so fine that he had to screw up his eyes to try to see them. 'I wish the lines on my fingers were bigger, then I could see them better,' he said.

Soon after this it was Eric's birthday. His Grandad gave him something that was an odd shape. It was wrapped in brown paper. There was a label on it. Eric's mother read it out to him: 'Here's something to help you see better, Eric. It will make things bigger. It's your extra eye!'

Eric didn't open the parcel straight away. First he felt the shape, to see if he could guess what his Grandad had given him. The parcel seemed to have a long handle inside, with a round, flat piece at the other end. Eric couldn't think what it might be. He opened it. Inside was – a magnifying glass.

There was a long handle with a round glass at the other end. Eric held the handle in his hand. He wondered why his Grandad had called it an extra eye. He looked through the glass. Then he really did have a surprise!

Suddenly things looked bigger! He held up his finger and looked at it through the magnifying glass. He could see all the curly lines curving all over his pink finger! He turned his hand over and looked at the back of it. The hairs on the back of his hand were much bigger, and his brown freckles were huge!

He went up close to the mirror and looked at his eye. What a giant blue eye! It was so enormous it was quite frightening!

'This is great!' said Eric. 'This is fantastic!' And off he went to look at everything again through his new magnifying glass!

Follow-up activities

o   Collect pictures of different tools and machines. Sort them into sets of lifting machines, cutting machines, carrying machines, digging machines, and so on.

Plasticine models

o   Make pictures of machines using squares, circles, rectangles and triangles cut from brightly coloured sticky paper.

o   Make drawings or take photographs of machines used at home, at school or in your neighbourhood. Use clay, dough or plasticine to make models of these familiar machines at work.

o   Invent your own machines to help you with jobs that need doing, e.g. tidying your bedroom or making sure you get to school on time.

hammer

saw

pincers

Or invent strange fantasy machines to help with more unusual tasks, e.g. catching a cloud or washing a dinosaur.

pliers

plane

chisel

screwdriver

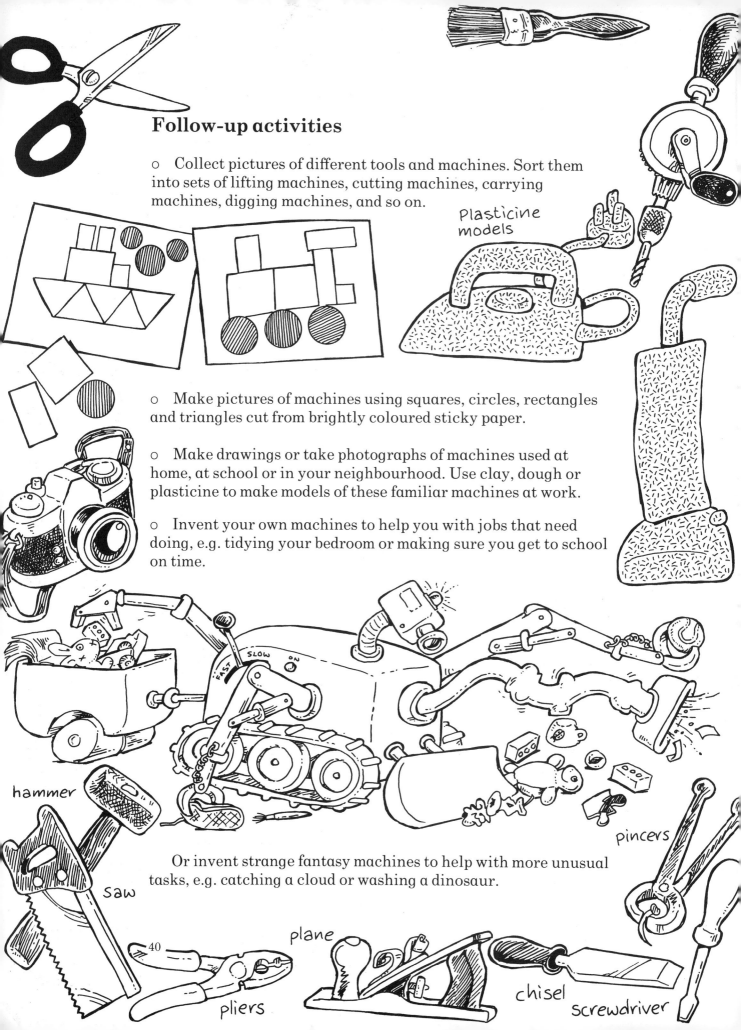

nail patterns

plane

balsa wood

dowling

crane

String

bent nail

nuts and bolts

Spanner

o   Make a collection of familiar tools and machines. Under adult supervision, children can be encouraged to experiment with these tools, e.g. hammering nails into wood, putting in screws with a screwdriver and cutting balsa wood with a saw.

o   Make nail pattern designs.

o   Use balsa wood to make simple models of ships, aeroplanes, machines and so on.

o   Collect old alarm clocks, radios and other household tools and machines which are no longer wanted or working. Under supervision, explore the secrets of their mechanisms.
N.B. All children should be warned about the dangers of tampering with electricity.

o   Use a magnifying glass to investigate tiny cogs and springs. This may lead you into a closer exploration of a world that is normally hidden from us, e.g. tiny insects, the weave of materials, finger prints and so on.

41

robots

I'm a little robot

Ronald Zachary Taylor

1 I'm a lit-tle ro-bot made of tin, Take my plug and
plug me in. Press the lit-tle switch and turn the knob,
Now I'm rea-dy, to tac-kle a-ny job. *Chorus* See my arms go
up and down, See my eyes go round and round. I can
jump and climb, I can walk and run. You and I can have some fun!

Anytime you need me give a clap,
I will waken from my nap.
Press the little switch and turn the knob,
Now I'm ready to tackle any job.

Chorus

Dum-a-diddle-bang-click, whizz and shake,
That's the happy sound I make,
Press the little switch and turn the knob,
Now I'm ready to tackle any job.

Chorus

Raju's robot
by Sara Strange

Raju's Mum was an inventor. She invented things that no one had ever made before. She invented machines that whirred, and machines that clanked, and machines with wheels that rumbled round and round.

Everyone came to Raju's Mum if they wanted a new machine invented. 'Can you make me a machine to take my dog for a walk?' asked Mrs Keen. 'Of course,' said Raju's Mum. She went into her workshop and tapped and banged and soon, there was the dog-walking machine ready for Mrs Keen.

'Can you invent a machine to make my flowers grow?' grumbled Mr Warburton. 'No problem,' said Raju's Mum. She went into her workshop and she hammered and she sawed and soon, there was the flower-growing machine, ready for Mr Warburton.

'Can you build me a machine to make the sun shine on my birthday?' said old Mrs Chapman. 'That's easy,' said Raju's Mum. She went into her workshop and she glued and she painted and soon, there was the sunshine machine ready for Mrs Chapman.

Raju sat on the floor of the workshop. She thought her Mum was very clever. Then she had an idea. 'Can you invent something for me?' she said.

'Now that,' said her mum, 'is much more difficult. I'm going to need some help.'

'I'll help, I'll help,' Raju almost shouted. 'Then we'll make you a robot to help tidy up your bedroom,' said Raju's Mum.

Soon they had collected a big pile of old cardboard boxes, plastic tubs and old cardboard rolls. Raju's Mum took down a pot of glue and a pair of shiny scissors from the top shelf.

'Now,' she said, 'We'll start with these two big boxes,' and she showed Raju how to glue the two ends together to make the robot's head and body.

Then they chose two plastic tubs. Raju spread more glue on the bottom of the tubs and pressed them on to the bottom of the biggest box. 'Now my robot's got two feet,' she laughed.

Next Raju's Mum helped her fix two cardboard rolls on the sides of the box. 'They look like long, straight arms,' said Raju.

In one corner of the workshop, Raju found some shiny silver paper. She carefully cut out some round shapes and stuck them on the front of the smaller box. 'One nose . . . one mouth . . . and one . . . two . . . eyes.'

At last the robot was finished. Raju ran over and gave her Mum a big kiss. 'Thank you for inventing something especially for me,' she said.

43

Follow-up activities

o Make collage robot pictures using shapes cut from silver foil. Glue on shiny buttons, springs and small cogs. What jobs could your robot help you with?

a simple circuit

o Make a large, 3D robot from cardboard boxes and other junk material. Use a can of paint to spray the robot silver. A simple circuit will light up the robot's eyes.

o Measure your robot with non-standard measures such as handspans and footsteps, and standard measures, i.e. centimetres and metres.

kitchen foil

paper plate, nails nuts, match box

o Stick seeds and small card shapes on to a firm base to make a robot picture or an abstract pattern. Cover the base with silver foil and press it around the raised shapes so your design stands out. Keep your foil picture as a wall decoration, or use it as a printing block to make wrapping paper, birthday cards and so on.

o Make robot masks from cylinders or card. Cut out eye shapes and cover the mask with pasta shapes, washers and milk bottle tops. Spray it silver.

egg box sections, tube tops, small boxes, paper clips

Can pulls, milk bottle tops, buttons, tubes

pasta shapes

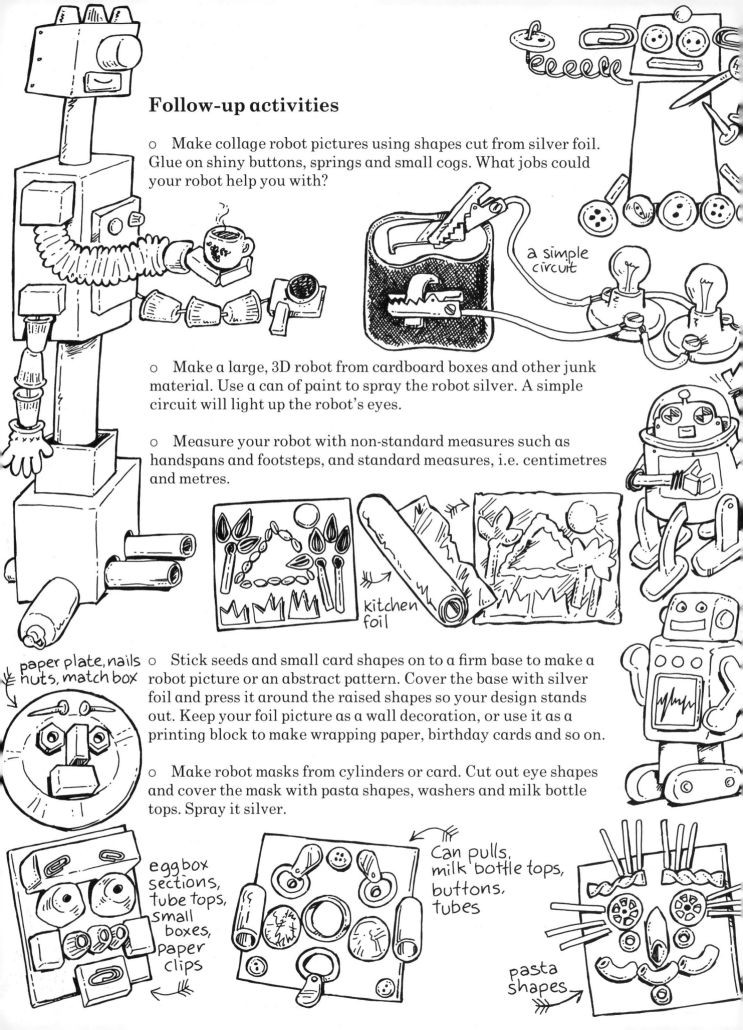

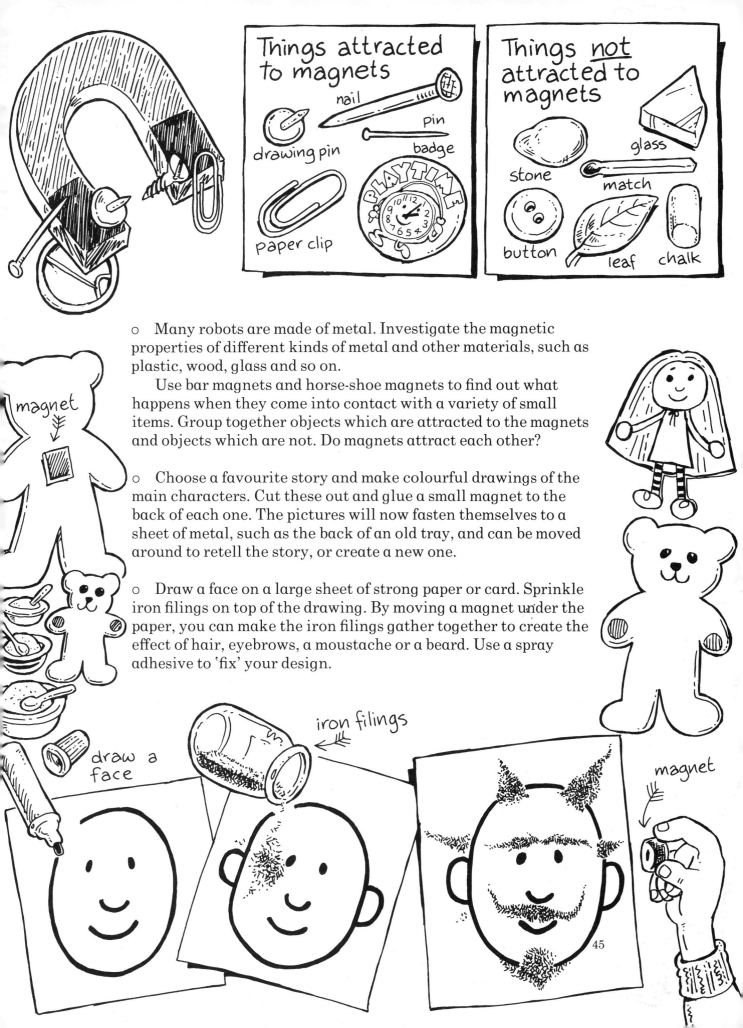

Things attracted to magnets

nail

pin

drawing pin

badge

PLAYTIME

paper clip

Things <u>not</u> attracted to magnets

glass

stone

match

button

leaf

chalk

o   Many robots are made of metal. Investigate the magnetic properties of different kinds of metal and other materials, such as plastic, wood, glass and so on.

Use bar magnets and horse-shoe magnets to find out what happens when they come into contact with a variety of small items. Group together objects which are attracted to the magnets and objects which are not. Do magnets attract each other?

o   Choose a favourite story and make colourful drawings of the main characters. Cut these out and glue a small magnet to the back of each one. The pictures will now fasten themselves to a sheet of metal, such as the back of an old tray, and can be moved around to retell the story, or create a new one.

o   Draw a face on a large sheet of strong paper or card. Sprinkle iron filings on top of the drawing. By moving a magnet under the paper, you can make the iron filings gather together to create the effect of hair, eyebrows, a moustache or a beard. Use a spray adhesive to 'fix' your design.

magnet

iron filings

draw a face

magnet

45

transport

Riding on my bike

Ronald Zachary Taylor

Dad-dies got a lor-ry   Mum-my drives a van
Grand-pa drives his mo-tor-car As safe-ly as he can.
Sis-ter sails a sail-ing boat, Bro-ther drives a train
Un-cle drives a big red bus And Grand-ma flies a 'plane.
Ev-'ry-bo-dy's hap-py driv-ing what they like, But
I'm the hap-piest one of all Rid-ing on my bike.___

Mr Baker's bike

by John Escott

Kenny and his parents had a new neighbour. The neighbour's
name was Mr Baker and he was a very friendly man. Kenny liked
him.

'Do you like my new bike, Mr Baker?' Kenny asked one day.

'Yes, I do, Kenny,' Mr Baker said. 'But did you know I have a
bike as well?'

Kenny was surprised. He knew Mr Baker had a car because he
had seen it, but he had never seen Mr Baker riding a bicycle.

'I only ride it on special occasions,' Mr Baker said. 'You see, it's a rather *special* bike.'

'A special bike?' Kenny said. 'Ooh, can I see it?'

So Mr Baker took Kenny up to the top of his garden where there was a large shed. Mr Baker opened the shed door. And inside was the strangest bike Kenny had ever seen.

It had one huge wheel in the front, and one tiny wheel at the back, and the pedals were fixed to the front wheel. And the saddle was a long, long way from the ground.

'What sort of bike is that?' gasped Kenny.

Mr Baker laughed. 'It's called a penny-farthing bike,' he said. 'It used to belong to my Grandfather.'

'A penny-farthing bike?' Kenny said. 'Why is it called that?'

'Because one wheel is big and the other is small,' Mr Baker said. 'You see, Kenny, years ago the penny was a much bigger coin than it is today.' He reached up and took an old tobacco tin from a shelf in the shed, then he opened it. 'Here's one for you to see.'

Kenny looked at the coin which Mr Baker took from the tin. 'It is bigger,' he said.

'Then there was a tiny coin called the farthing,' Mr Baker said. 'Look, I have one of those as well.' And he took a tiny coin, no bigger than Kenny's thumbnail, from the tobacco tin.

'One big, one small!' Kenny laughed. 'Like the wheels on the bike. Now I see why it was called a penny-farthing bike.'

Even so, it seemed a strange sort of bicycle for anybody to have. Kenny couldn't imagine when Mr Baker would dare to ride it.

'Don't people laugh at you when you ride your bike, Mr Baker?' Kenny asked.

Mr Baker smiled. 'Yes, they do, Kenny. But that is exactly what I want them to do.'

Kenny couldn't understand why Mr Baker should want people to laugh at him but he didn't say anything.

It was several weeks later, on the day of the town carnival, that Kenny discovered when Mr Baker rode his strange bike and why he liked people to laugh at him.

There, right at the front of the carnival parade, was Mr Baker on his penny-farthing bike – dressed like a clown!

'Hello, Kenny!' Mr Baker called, waving.

'Hello, Mr Baker!' Kenny shouted back. 'That's Mr Baker on his penny-farthing bike,' he told everybody in the crowd who were watching. 'Do *you* know why it's called a penny-farthing? I do.'

And so do we, don't we?

Follow-up activities

o   Experiment to find out which shapes roll best – spheres, cones, cylinders, cubes or cuboids. Group together sets of shapes which will roll and shapes which will not roll.

o   Collect pictures of different kinds of vehicles. Group them according to the number of wheels they possess, the jobs they do, or whether they move in the air, on land or in water.

o   Look at the tread on a large tyre. What is it for? Make rubbings of the pattern. Paint the tyres of toy vehicles to make tracks across sheets of paper. Use different colours and different tyres to make an attractive tyre pattern.

o   Make large models of different vehicles from junk material: an aeroplane, a milkfloat, a tractor, a dust cart, an ambulance, a police motor bike.

o   Make a balloon rocket from a balloon, a straw and a length of fine string or cotton. Thread the string or cotton through the straw. Blow up the balloon and pinch the end to prevent the air escaping. Tape the straw to the balloon. Slide the balloon to one end of the string. Stretch the string tightly across the room and release the end of the balloon.

48

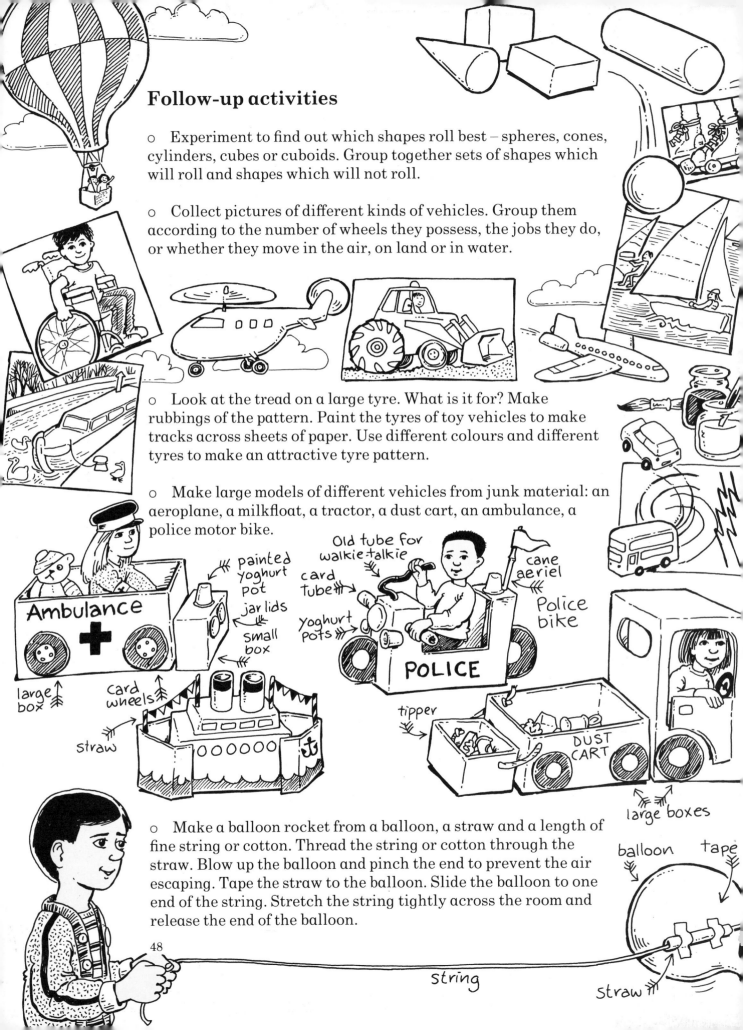

o   Make a large rocket by taping large cardboard boxes together and fastening a roll of corrugated card around them. Add a conical-shaped capsule of card to the top. Spray the rocket silver and decorate it with foil shapes and milk bottle tops.

o   Make a pretend passport. Draw a self-portrait and stick it on one side of a folded piece of card. On the other side, write your name, age and address.

o   Collect holiday brochures and cut out pictures of places you would like to visit. These could be used as a basis to find out more about particular countries, or parts of the world.

o   Find out more about the first vehicles to be built, the first train, car, bicycle and rocket.

first manned space rocket

first passenger train

first plane

o   Invent a new kind of vehicle which will allow you to travel on the land, under water and up into space. Draw or paint pictures of the design and talk about the adventures you have in your new vehicle.

My Passport
Name_____
Age _____
Height_____
Eyes_____
Hair_____

toys and games

Going out to play

Chris Warde

I'm going out to play.
What will I do today?
I think I'm going to play ...
Riding on my bike.
    Whistle ...
Ting a ling a ling a ling. (*4 times*)

... Driving in my car.
    Whistle ...
Beep a beep a beep a beep. (*4 times*)

... Bat and ball, bat and ball.
    Whistle ...
TOK! wheeeee ... POP! (*4 times*)

... With my skipping rope.
    Whistle ...
Skippa skippa skippa hop. (*4 times*)

The home-made bobby-dazzler
by Pam Ayres

Dad worked at the sawmill but the sawmill closed. So Dad was at home all the time now. He didn't seem very happy.

'What's the matter with Dad?' Sam asked his Mum.

'Dad's lost his job, Sammy,' said Mum. 'Poor old Dad misses going to work every day. And it means we haven't much money to spend because Dad's getting no wages.'

Sam looked worried. 'Will I still get the fire engine I wanted for my birthday, Mum?' he asked.

'You'll have to ask Dad about that,' she replied.

Sam asked his Dad. 'I'm sorry, Sam. We don't have as much money as we used to have. But tell me about the sort of fire engine you want anyway.'

'It's in the toy shop window,' Sam began. 'It's fantastic. It's big and red with silver bits, ladders and a hose pipe at the back.'

'How many wheels?' asked Dad, looking a bit thoughtful now.

'Oh lots!' cried Sam. 'Lots, on each side!'

That night, after Sam went to bed he heard strange sounds coming from downstairs, the scraping of a saw, somebody banging with a hammer and all sorts of drilling noises. 'I wonder what's going on?' Sam thought as he drifted off to sleep.

A few days later, Sam was sitting on the step and Dad came out with a big bag. 'Look here, Sam,' he said, and sat down too. 'Do you know that fire engine in the toy shop?' Sam nodded. 'Well, we can't afford it, and that's that.' Sam looked disappointed.

'But,' Dad went on, 'I've had a go at making you one. I think you'll agree it's quite a bobby-dazzler! The only thing I couldn't make you was the hose pipe because that's rubber. I'll take you to town today and get one at the toy shop.' Sam took out his new fire engine and gave Dad a big hug.

Later on they went to the toy shop with the fire engine. There was a boy with his Mum and together with the lady behind the counter they were examining something broken. Sam looked. It was a fire engine! One of the smart plastic ones in the window, that he had wanted before Dad made him the bobby-dazzler! The other little boy was very upset, pointing out to the lady where the silver bits had come off and wheels come loose. Sam took out his own fire engine to check that his was all right. As he stood holding it, the lady at the counter noticed him.

'*That's* what I wish I could find for my shop,' she said. 'Big, strong fire engines that don't break, like yours.'

Sam looked up proudly. 'My Dad made it.'

'Oh,' said the lady in an interested voice. 'And is this your Daddy here?'

'Yes,' replied Sam. He hurried off to look for the reel of hose he needed. Dad and the lady were talking, and when they left the shop later, Dad seemed very pleased.

On the way home Sam asked, 'What did the toy shop lady want, Dad?'

'Well,' said Dad, smiling, 'she wants me to make some more wooden fire engines to sell in the toy shop!'

'Is it because she liked mine?' Sam asked.

'Yes,' said Dad, laughing. 'She thought yours was a real bobby-dazzler!'

building blocks

cut out holes

jigsaws

shoe box

posting box

Follow-up activities

o Make a jig-saw puzzle from a magazine picture glued to strong card and cut into large pieces.

o Make a posting box.

o Make a necklace from cotton reels or rolled up newspaper cut into short lengths.

newspaper

2. Cut into lengths

necklace

1. Roll up and glue end

o Make a cotton-reel snake.

3. Paint and thread with string

o Design your own sewing cards.

Snake

thin card

holes

cotton reels

o Make string puppets from card.

String (tape end)

Cut out two puppet shapes from material

o Make finger puppets from felt or card.

thick card

String Puppet

o Make glove puppets from felt or old socks.

Use pens or glue on fabric for eyes, mouth nose, etc.

add string head a arms

paper fastene

sew edges together

52

glove puppets

leave open

finger puppets

leave open

Sew two felt finger shapes together then decorate with pens and material scrap lotto

pin wheel

o Make a simple lotto game.

o Make a pin wheel.

Square of paper.

1   2   3

Cut halfway down diagonals turn in corners and secure with a paper fastener add a stick

o Make a kite from straws and tissue paper.

o Make pom-pom animals.

Wrap wool round two card rings

2. Cut through loops

3. tie between rings with wool and remove them

4. glue on felt eyes, feet etc.

thin string or cotton

tissue paper

glue on straws

tissue paper

pom-pom caterpillar

o Make a pouch.

Circle of cloth

Punch out an odd number of holes thread string through

o Make a peep theatre in a shoe box.

Cut out back of box and cover it with tissue paper.

Suspend characters and scenery from the lid or stick them to the bottom with flaps

peep hole

53

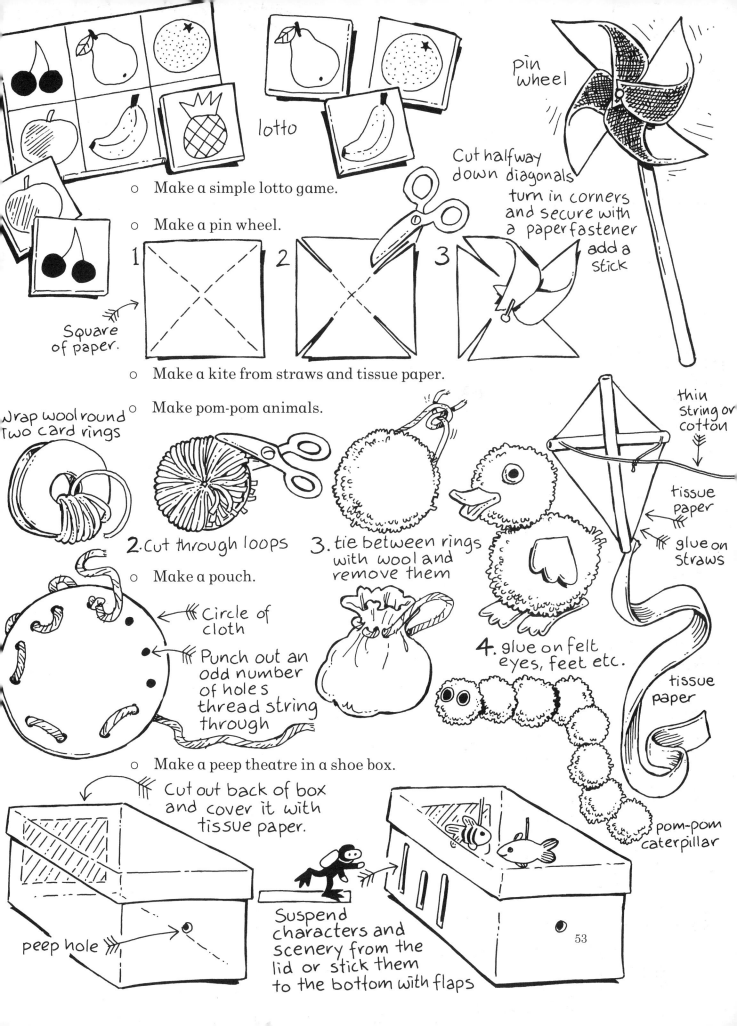

let's pretend

Five fierce dragons

Five fierce dragons playing on the shore
One fell down and that left four.
Four fierce dragons said 'Let's have tea'
One had a cold and that left three.
Three fierce dragons went to the zoo
One stayed behind and that left two.
Two fierce dragons looking for some fun
One got the giggles and that left one.
One fierce dragon sitting in the sun
Went to sleep and that left none.

Patricia Taylor

The explorer

I would like a great big ladder
To climb into the sky;
I would like to turn the rain on
When the earth is hot and dry;
I'd let a thousand snowflakes fall
Floating to the ground;
I'd ride a bird, and chase the wind
And blow the clouds around.
I'd paint a rainbow, catch a star,
The sun's bright flames I'd see;
Then the Man-in-the-Moon would come in a balloon,
And we'd both drift home for tea.

J M Godfrey

Soolee and the dragon

by Patricia Taylor

Soolee made a kite at school. It was made from paper and sticks and on it she had painted a dragon with a long tail and wings. It was a happy dragon with green eyes and a huge red tongue sticking out of a big, laughing mouth. At bedtime Soolee hung her kite on the wall with the dragon's face laughing down at her.

'I wish I could fly through the sky like the dragon on my kite,' murmured Soolee as she fell off to sleep.

'I can take you flying,' said the voice of the dragon. 'Climb on my back.'

Soolee sat up. 'Can you really?' she said. She climbed out of bed and, wrapping her arms around the dragon's neck, she held on tight as they flew out of the open window. Soolee wanted to clap her hands with happiness but she was frightened of falling off. They flew over the roof tops and she heard a loud noise.

'What's that?' Soolee asked. The dragon swooped down and she saw the blue light of an ambulance hurrying to the hospital.

'Shall we take a ride on a bus?' the dragon chuckled and he promptly landed with a loud thud on top of a big red bus. The bus stopped.

'Oh quickly,' shouted Soolee. 'The people are getting out to see what's happened.' With a swish of his tail and a flapping of wings, the dragon quickly took off.

A fire engine was speeding down the street with its lights flashing and its bell clanging. 'How about a ride on the fire engine instead,' said the dragon, and landed on top of its ladder.

When they came to the fire Soolee cried, 'Oh, isn't there anything we can do?'

'Yes,' said the dragon. 'Not only can I breathe out fire, I can also blow very hard. Watch . . .' He took a big breath and blew as hard as he could at the fire. The fire went out just like the candles on a birthday cake.

'That's wonderful,' shouted Soolee. 'Can we see something else?'

'That's enough excitement for one night,' said the dragon, and he flapped his wings and carried Soolee home.

'What a lot to tell my friends,' thought Soolee sleepily, as she snuggled up in bed. 'But I don't think they'll believe me'. Do you?

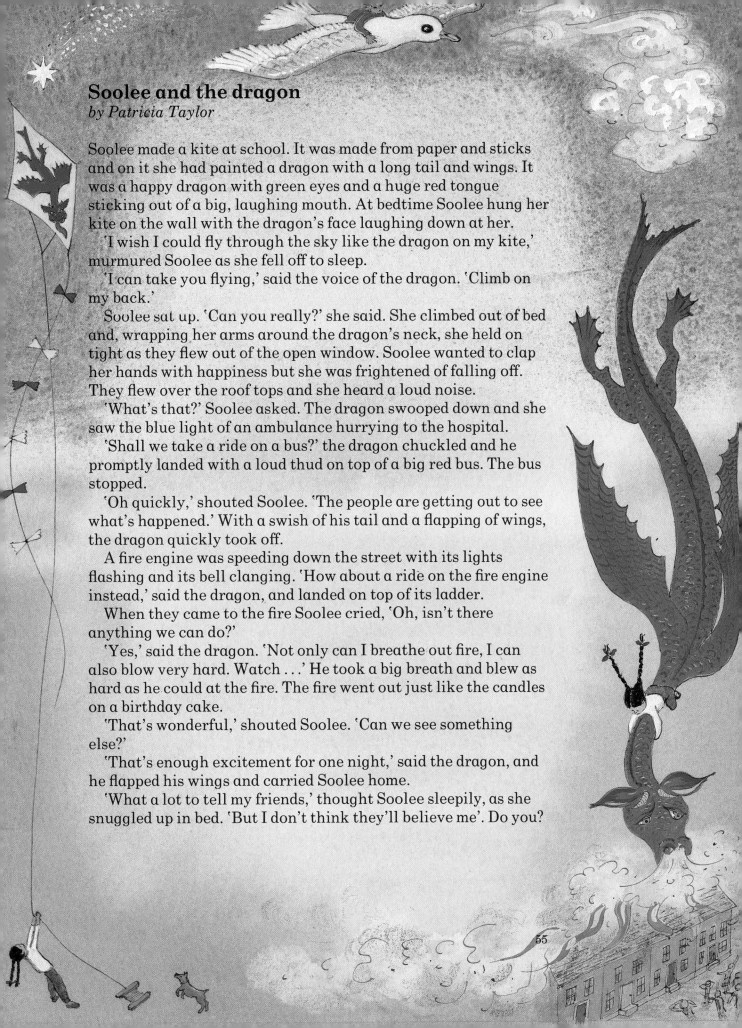

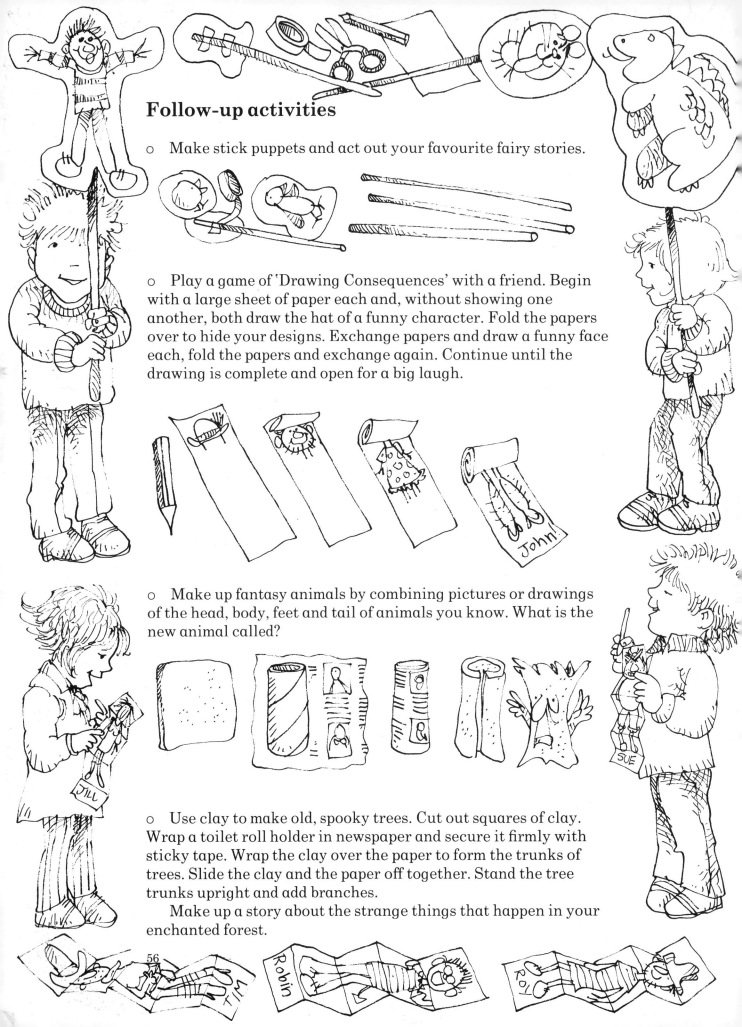

Follow-up activities

o   Make stick puppets and act out your favourite fairy stories.

o   Play a game of 'Drawing Consequences' with a friend. Begin with a large sheet of paper each and, without showing one another, both draw the hat of a funny character. Fold the papers over to hide your designs. Exchange papers and draw a funny face each, fold the papers and exchange again. Continue until the drawing is complete and open for a big laugh.

o   Make up fantasy animals by combining pictures or drawings of the head, body, feet and tail of animals you know. What is the new animal called?

o   Use clay to make old, spooky trees. Cut out squares of clay. Wrap a toilet roll holder in newspaper and secure it firmly with sticky tape. Wrap the clay over the paper to form the trunks of trees. Slide the clay and the paper off together. Stand the tree trunks upright and add branches.

Make up a story about the strange things that happen in your enchanted forest.

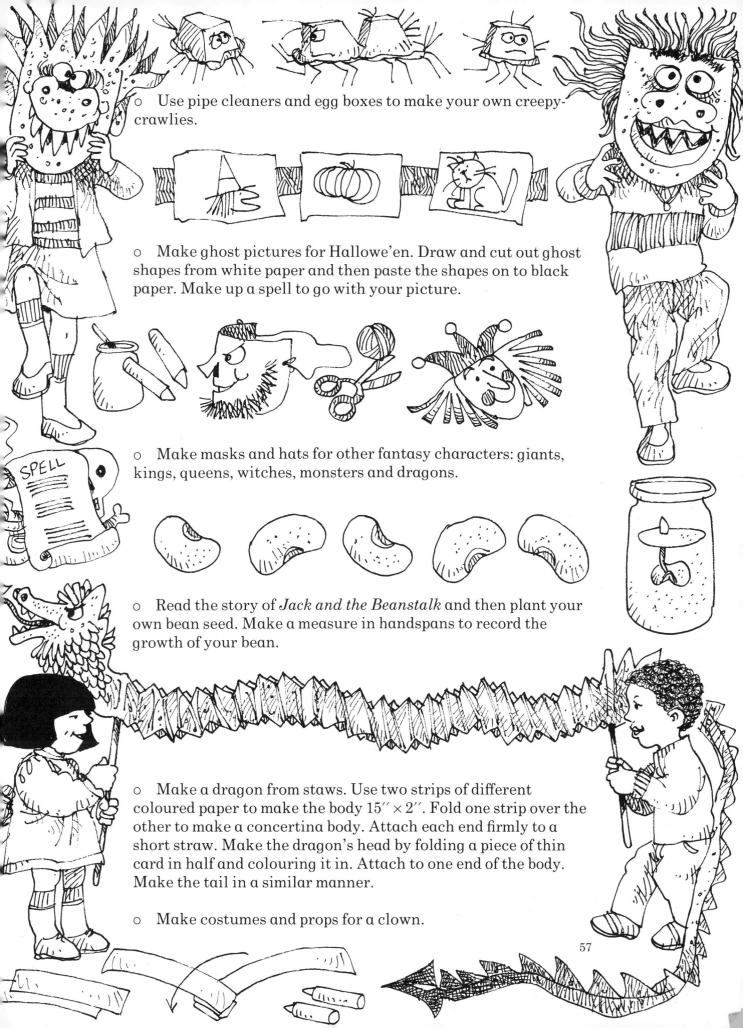

o   Use pipe cleaners and egg boxes to make your own creepy-crawlies.

o   Make ghost pictures for Hallowe'en. Draw and cut out ghost shapes from white paper and then paste the shapes on to black paper. Make up a spell to go with your picture.

o   Make masks and hats for other fantasy characters: giants, kings, queens, witches, monsters and dragons.

o   Read the story of *Jack and the Beanstalk* and then plant your own bean seed. Make a measure in handspans to record the growth of your bean.

o   Make a dragon from staws. Use two strips of different coloured paper to make the body 15″ × 2″. Fold one strip over the other to make a concertina body. Attach each end firmly to a short straw. Make the dragon's head by folding a piece of thin card in half and colouring it in. Attach to one end of the body. Make the tail in a similar manner.

o   Make costumes and props for a clown.

water

Water

Ronald Zachary Taylor

1 Fall-ing from the sky run-ning down the drain-pipes
Fill-ing all the gut-ters as it tries to get a-way
Fill-ing all the lakes fill-ing all the duck-ponds
Gush-ing down the ri-ver on its way to the sea. 2 Drip! Swish!
Splash! goes the wa-ter Where does it come from Where does it go?
Drip! Swish! Splash! goes the wa-ter Where does it come from
Where oh where does it go?

Susie's bathtime journey

by Guy Hutchins

One day, Susie was having her bath. She splashed the water this
way and that way to make a storm. Splosh – and then splish –
huge waves spattered on the sides and crashed back to the middle.
The really big ones tickled her tummy when they broke against it.
Some of the water went on the floor.

'Careful, Susie,' said Dad.

'Sorry, Dad,' said Susie, 'I didn't think it would go over.'

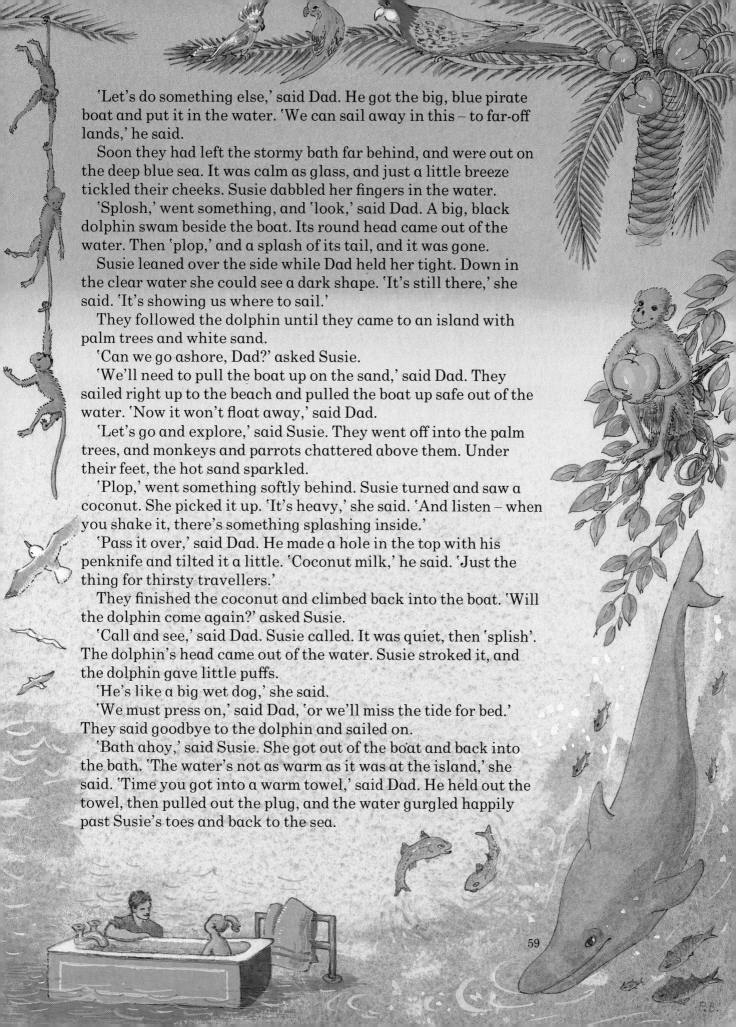

'Let's do something else,' said Dad. He got the big, blue pirate boat and put it in the water. 'We can sail away in this – to far-off lands,' he said.

Soon they had left the stormy bath far behind, and were out on the deep blue sea. It was calm as glass, and just a little breeze tickled their cheeks. Susie dabbled her fingers in the water.

'Splosh,' went something, and 'look,' said Dad. A big, black dolphin swam beside the boat. Its round head came out of the water. Then 'plop,' and a splash of its tail, and it was gone.

Susie leaned over the side while Dad held her tight. Down in the clear water she could see a dark shape. 'It's still there,' she said. 'It's showing us where to sail.'

They followed the dolphin until they came to an island with palm trees and white sand.

'Can we go ashore, Dad?' asked Susie.

'We'll need to pull the boat up on the sand,' said Dad. They sailed right up to the beach and pulled the boat up safe out of the water. 'Now it won't float away,' said Dad.

'Let's go and explore,' said Susie. They went off into the palm trees, and monkeys and parrots chattered above them. Under their feet, the hot sand sparkled.

'Plop,' went something softly behind. Susie turned and saw a coconut. She picked it up. 'It's heavy,' she said. 'And listen – when you shake it, there's something splashing inside.'

'Pass it over,' said Dad. He made a hole in the top with his penknife and tilted it a little. 'Coconut milk,' he said. 'Just the thing for thirsty travellers.'

They finished the coconut and climbed back into the boat. 'Will the dolphin come again?' asked Susie.

'Call and see,' said Dad. Susie called. It was quiet, then 'splash'. The dolphin's head came out of the water. Susie stroked it, and the dolphin gave little puffs.

'He's like a big wet dog,' she said.

'We must press on,' said Dad, 'or we'll miss the tide for bed.' They said goodbye to the dolphin and sailed on.

'Bath ahoy,' said Susie. She got out of the boat and back into the bath. 'The water's not as warm as it was at the island,' she said. 'Time you got into a warm towel,' said Dad. He held out the towel, then pulled out the plug, and the water gurgled happily past Susie's toes and back to the sea.

Follow-up activities

o   Make an 'all about water' mobile.

o   Paint water pictures.

o   Make a fishing game using card, paper clips and a magnet tied to a length of dowel rod. Encourage young children to recognise the numbers on the fish they catch. Older children may be able to add up their scores.

o   Make a collection of familiar objects. Take turns to pick up an object and guess whether it will float or sink. Use a large bowl of water to check your guesses.

date box ship

plastic

paper

wo

o   Make boats from a variety of materials: wood, paper, foil, Plasticine. Which boat floats longest and furthest? Which boat will carry the most cargo?

60

o   Make bubbles by blowing into a mixture of washing-up liquid and water with a straw.

Experiment with other ways of making bubbles with and without soap. Which methods are most successful?

o   Which way do bubbles move in water?

o   Make your own spirit level, using a tall, clear, plastic bottle almost filled with water and find flat surfaces to test it on.

o   Find or make a puddle on a safe, flat, hard surface. Draw round the outer edge with chalk. As the water evaporates, mark where the new outer limits of the puddle are. (How often you do this will depend on the rate of evaporation.) Do puddles change their shape as they dry out? Where does all the water go?

o   Make your own canal scene.

sherbet

the sea

That's the life for me

Traditional
Arrangement by Barry Gibson

When I was one, I ate a bun,
The day I went to sea.
I jumped on board a pirate ship (*Jump up high*)

And the captain said to me,
'I'm going this way, that way (*Sway from side to side*)

Forwards and backwards
Over the deep blue sea.
A bottle of rum to fill my tum (*Pat tummy*)

That's the life for me.'

When I was two, I buckled my shoes (*Touch shoe*)
The day I went to sea . . .

When I was three, I grazed my knee (*Rub knee*)
The day I went to sea . . .

When I was four, I knocked at the door (*Knock at door*)
The day I went to sea . . . (*Make up your own verses*)

P.B

Pirate gold
by Guy Hutchins

Winston was playing pirates. He made a fierce-looking eye patch with some elastic and black cardboard. Then he folded a newspaper this way and that way to make a pirate hat. He looked in the mirror and scowled a wicked pirate face.

'I look like a pirate,' he thought. 'Now all I need is something to do.' He found a big cardboard box and climbed in. This is my pirate boat,' he said. 'I'll row away and find some treasure.' He pulled hard on the oars. His Mum came in.

'You look fierce,' she said.

'I'm a pirate,' said Winston. 'Let's dig for some treasure!'

They put on their coats and boots and rowed out into the garden. It was cold. Winston shivered. They went to the shed, and Mum found the spade she used for planting seeds. Winston took the spade and began to dig. It was hard work pushing the spade into the ground. He saw something move in the ground. It was a wriggly, pink earthworm. Winston picked it up and put it beside the hole.

'Wriggle away, worm,' he said, 'and stay away from the spade.' The worm wriggled back into the ground. Winston dug some more. There were stones that crunched on the spade – and bits of broken flower pot – but no treasure.

'I didn't know it was such hard work being a pirate,' he said. He was getting hungry. 'I'll dig a little bit more, then I'll go and ask Mum for a biscuit,' he thought.

He pushed the spade into the ground. There was a clinking sound. It was different from the other noises. He pushed some more, and there it was again – chink! Winston looked in the hole. There was something gleaming at the bottom.

'I've found some treasure,' he said. 'Now I'm a real pirate.' He bent down closer and looked. The treasure sparkled back at him. He picked it up and brushed off the earth. It was a gold ring! Winston ran to the kitchen.

'Mum,' he shouted. 'Look!'

'Where did you find it?' asked Mum.

'In the treasure place. Where you told me to dig.'

'It's my gold ring. I've looked everywhere for it. I must have lost it when I was planting seeds.'

'I'm glad you told me to dig there,' said Winston.

'So am I,' said Mum. 'What a clever pirate you are.' Winston and his Mum went down to the shop. She bought him a big bag of gold coins, all filled with chocolate.

'Pirate gold,' she said, 'for the bravest pirate in all the world.'

63

Follow-up activities

o   Create a sea-side scene in a large tray. Include a lighthouse made from a washing-up liquid bottle. A simple circuit will light the bulb at the top of the lighthouse.

o   Make a sea garden. Collect shells, feathers, cones, beads, pebbles, dried leaves, ferns and flowers. Put a mixture of washing powder plus a little water (to make a stiff dough) into a flat shallow container. Stick the collection of leaves and shells into the mixture and sprinkle the base with gravel or coloured chippings (these are very cheap from a shop which sells tropical fish).

   Make small, brightly coloured fish and stick them on to pieces of straws. These can then be positioned between the shells and plants.

   The mixture should harden in approximately 15 minutes.

o   Make a Treasure Island. Use a base of plywood or strong card. Create hills from papier maché and a beach from sand sprinkled over glue. When this has dried, paint the island and the sea. Add figures, boats and buildings made from plasticine.

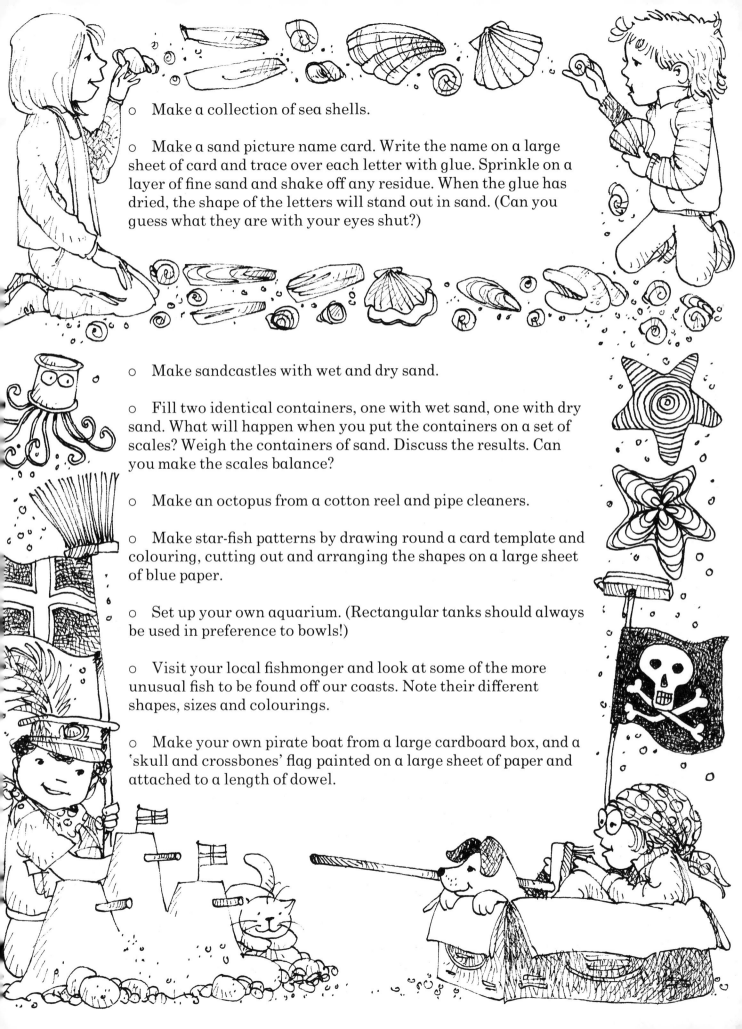

o   Make a collection of sea shells.

o   Make a sand picture name card. Write the name on a large sheet of card and trace over each letter with glue. Sprinkle on a layer of fine sand and shake off any residue. When the glue has dried, the shape of the letters will stand out in sand. (Can you guess what they are with your eyes shut?)

o   Make sandcastles with wet and dry sand.

o   Fill two identical containers, one with wet sand, one with dry sand. What will happen when you put the containers on a set of scales? Weigh the containers of sand. Discuss the results. Can you make the scales balance?

o   Make an octopus from a cotton reel and pipe cleaners.

o   Make star-fish patterns by drawing round a card template and colouring, cutting out and arranging the shapes on a large sheet of blue paper.

o   Set up your own aquarium. (Rectangular tanks should always be used in preference to bowls!)

o   Visit your local fishmonger and look at some of the more unusual fish to be found off our coasts. Note their different shapes, sizes and colourings.

o   Make your own pirate boat from a large cardboard box, and a 'skull and crossbones' flag painted on a large sheet of paper and attached to a length of dowel.

weather

Blow wind, blow free, blow for me!

Miss Dolly takes in washing
For neighbours and for friends,
She washes shirts and dresses,
She washes odds and ends.

Dripping dropping washing,
All around her flat,
Dripping dropping washing,
Going splish, splosh, splat.

But where's the wind?
Oh where's the wind?
Where's the wind today?
Has he gone away for ever?
Has he gone away to stay?
Why no, the wind's just taking
a little holiday.

Blow wind, blow free,
Blow for me –
Whoooosh, whoooo, wheeee!

Now there's washing in the garden,
Pegged out firmly on the line,
For the wind is blowing nicely
And everything is fine.

No more dripping dropping washing
All around her flat,
No more dripping dropping washing
Going splish, splosh, splat.

Angela Garner

66

P.B.

Winter

Winter's when –
Pipes freeze;
Noses sneeze;
Twigs snap;
Lips chap;
Birds hide;
Feet slide;
Coats duffle;
Scarves muffle;
Tears quiver;
Legs shiver;
Can't run;
No sun –
Brr-rrr!

I Egan

Shake your hands, everybody

Sandra Kerr

Shake your hands ev-'ry-bod-y, ev-'ry-bod-y shake your hands Ev-'ry-
bod-y shake your hands to-geth-er For it
won't do an-y harm and it 'll help to keep you warm In the

cold   and   crisp - y
wild   and   win - try
sleet   and   snow - y
bleak   and   blow - y
brisk   and   breez - y
frost   and   freez - y
coughs   and   sneez - y

wea - ther!

Clap your hands . . .

Wave your arms . . .

Stamp your feet . . .

Follow-up activities

o Make your own weather chart to record the weather each day.

Mon	Tues	Wed	Thurs	Fri	Sat	Sun	Mon
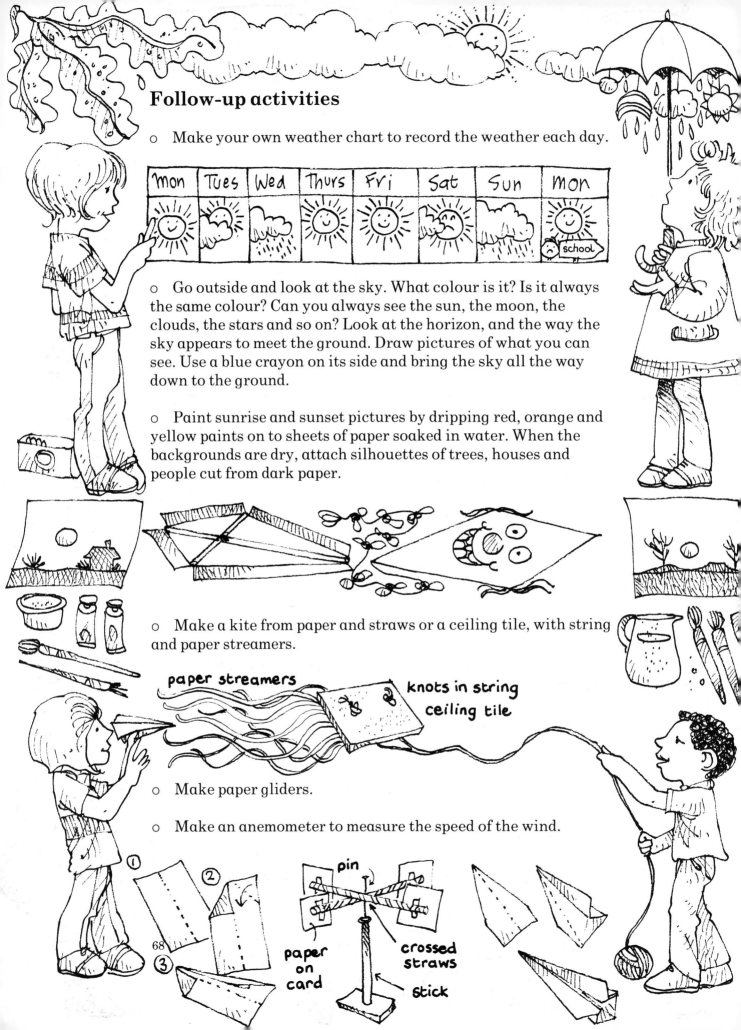

o Go outside and look at the sky. What colour is it? Is it always the same colour? Can you always see the sun, the moon, the clouds, the stars and so on? Look at the horizon, and the way the sky appears to meet the ground. Draw pictures of what you can see. Use a blue crayon on its side and bring the sky all the way down to the ground.

o Paint sunrise and sunset pictures by dripping red, orange and yellow paints on to sheets of paper soaked in water. When the backgrounds are dry, attach silhouettes of trees, houses and people cut from dark paper.

o Make a kite from paper and straws or a ceiling tile, with string and paper streamers.

paper streamers

knots in string
ceiling tile

o Make paper gliders.

o Make an anemometer to measure the speed of the wind.

pin

paper
on
card

crossed
straws

stick

68

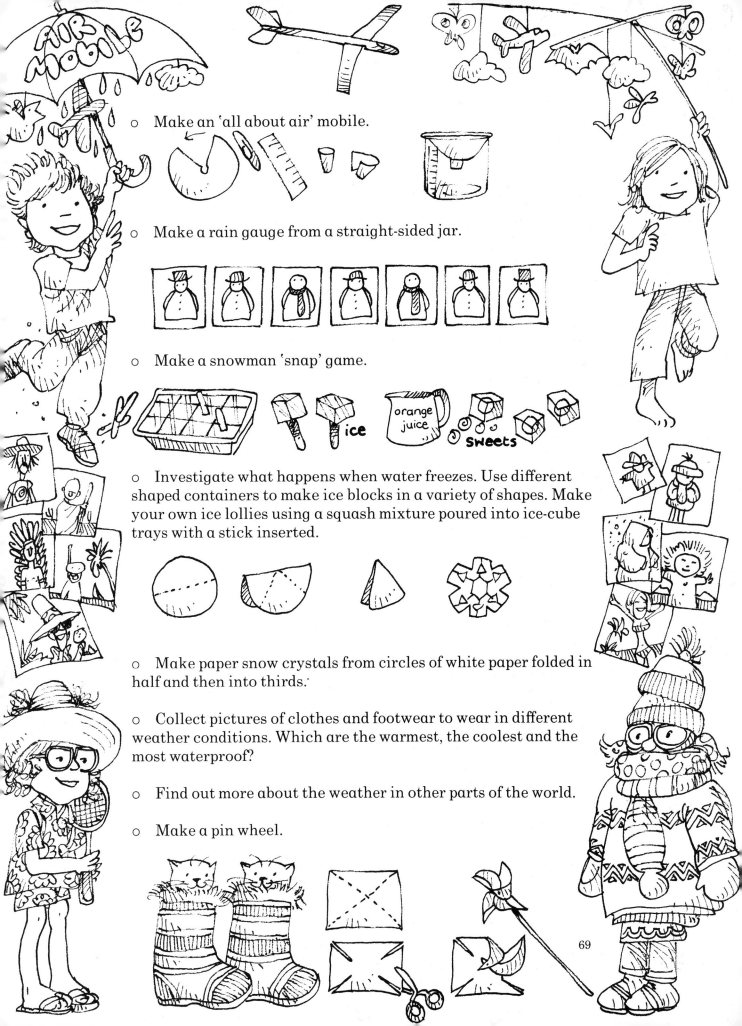

o   Make an 'all about air' mobile.

o   Make a rain gauge from a straight-sided jar.

o   Make a snowman 'snap' game.

o   Investigate what happens when water freezes. Use different shaped containers to make ice blocks in a variety of shapes. Make your own ice lollies using a squash mixture poured into ice-cube trays with a stick inserted.

o   Make paper snow crystals from circles of white paper folded in half and then into thirds.

o   Collect pictures of clothes and footwear to wear in different weather conditions. Which are the warmest, the coolest and the most waterproof?

o   Find out more about the weather in other parts of the world.

o   Make a pin wheel.

growing things

Here is a tree

Here is a tree with its leaves turned brown.
(Stretch your arms out like the branches)

Here comes the wind to blow the leaves down.
Whoooooo! Whoooooo!
(Make a noise like the wind)

Blow wind, blow, till the leaves whirl round,
(Shake you arms about in the wind)

Fluttering, floating, down to the ground,
(Wriggle your fingers like leaves floating to the ground)

Softly they fall, with hardly a sound.

Mary Kalemkerian

Lucy and the scarecrow
by Judy Taylor

Lucy felt happy. As she walked by Grandpa she gave a little hop and a skip. It was autumn time, and now that she was bigger, she was going to help Grandpa in his allotment.

'You're very bouncy today, Lucy,' laughed Grandpa.

Lucy ran ahead. She loved the feel of the fresh wind rushing through her hair. 'I'm a bird flying, Grandpa. Watch me. Wheee.'

Everywhere Lucy looked there were piles of autumn leaves fallen from the trees. She gathered great armfuls and threw them into the air. Then she danced round and round, as the leaves fluttered down, red, orange and gold. She landed with a dizzy bump on the ground.

'Look, Grandpa, what are these?' Lucy asked, as she picked up some cool, brown nuts from under the leaves.

'They are conkers, from that tall chestnut tree,' Grandpa smiled. 'I used to thread a string through them, and have conker fights when I was a boy. Feel how smooth and shiny they are.'

Lucy put the conkers into her tracksuit pocket. Then she giggled. She couldn't imagine her Grandpa little.

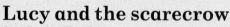

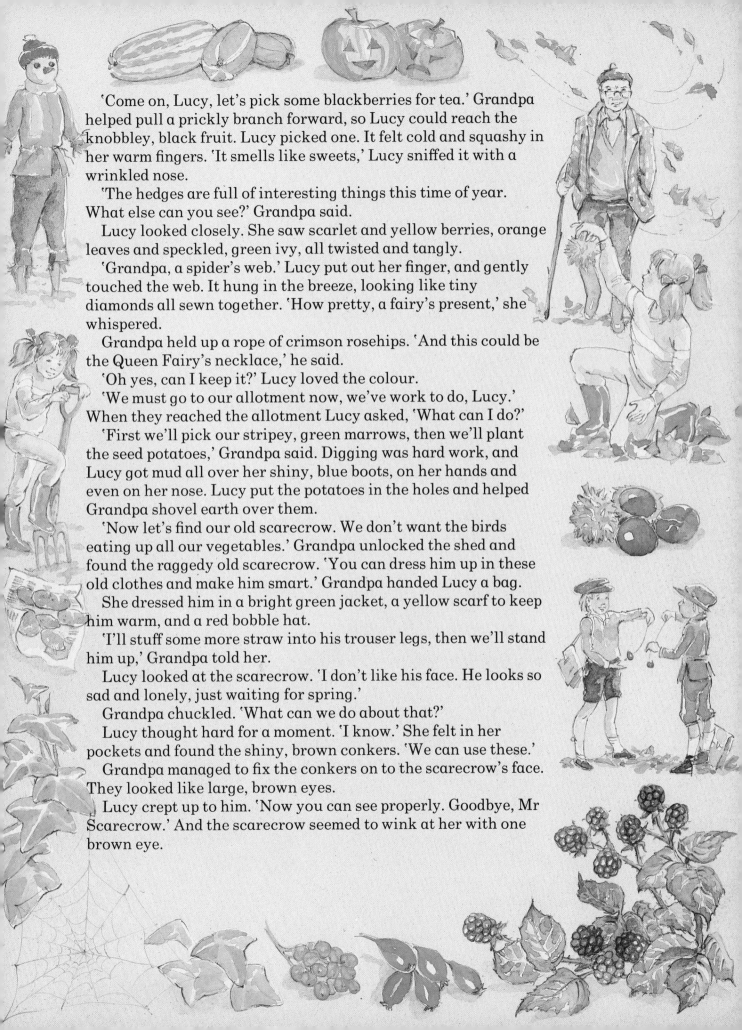

'Come on, Lucy, let's pick some blackberries for tea.' Grandpa helped pull a prickly branch forward, so Lucy could reach the knobbley, black fruit. Lucy picked one. It felt cold and squashy in her warm fingers. 'It smells like sweets,' Lucy sniffed it with a wrinkled nose.

'The hedges are full of interesting things this time of year. What else can you see?' Grandpa said.

Lucy looked closely. She saw scarlet and yellow berries, orange leaves and speckled, green ivy, all twisted and tangly.

'Grandpa, a spider's web.' Lucy put out her finger, and gently touched the web. It hung in the breeze, looking like tiny diamonds all sewn together. 'How pretty, a fairy's present,' she whispered.

Grandpa held up a rope of crimson rosehips. 'And this could be the Queen Fairy's necklace,' he said.

'Oh yes, can I keep it?' Lucy loved the colour.

'We must go to our allotment now, we've work to do, Lucy.' When they reached the allotment Lucy asked, 'What can I do?'

'First we'll pick our stripey, green marrows, then we'll plant the seed potatoes,' Grandpa said. Digging was hard work, and Lucy got mud all over her shiny, blue boots, on her hands and even on her nose. Lucy put the potatoes in the holes and helped Grandpa shovel earth over them.

'Now let's find our old scarecrow. We don't want the birds eating up all our vegetables.' Grandpa unlocked the shed and found the raggedy old scarecrow. 'You can dress him up in these old clothes and make him smart.' Grandpa handed Lucy a bag.

She dressed him in a bright green jacket, a yellow scarf to keep him warm, and a red bobble hat.

'I'll stuff some more straw into his trouser legs, then we'll stand him up,' Grandpa told her.

Lucy looked at the scarecrow. 'I don't like his face. He looks so sad and lonely, just waiting for spring.'

Grandpa chuckled. 'What can we do about that?'

Lucy thought hard for a moment. 'I know.' She felt in her pockets and found the shiny, brown conkers. 'We can use these.'

Grandpa managed to fix the conkers on to the scarecrow's face. They looked like large, brown eyes.

Lucy crept up to him. 'Now you can see properly. Goodbye, Mr Scarecrow.' And the scarecrow seemed to wink at her with one brown eye.

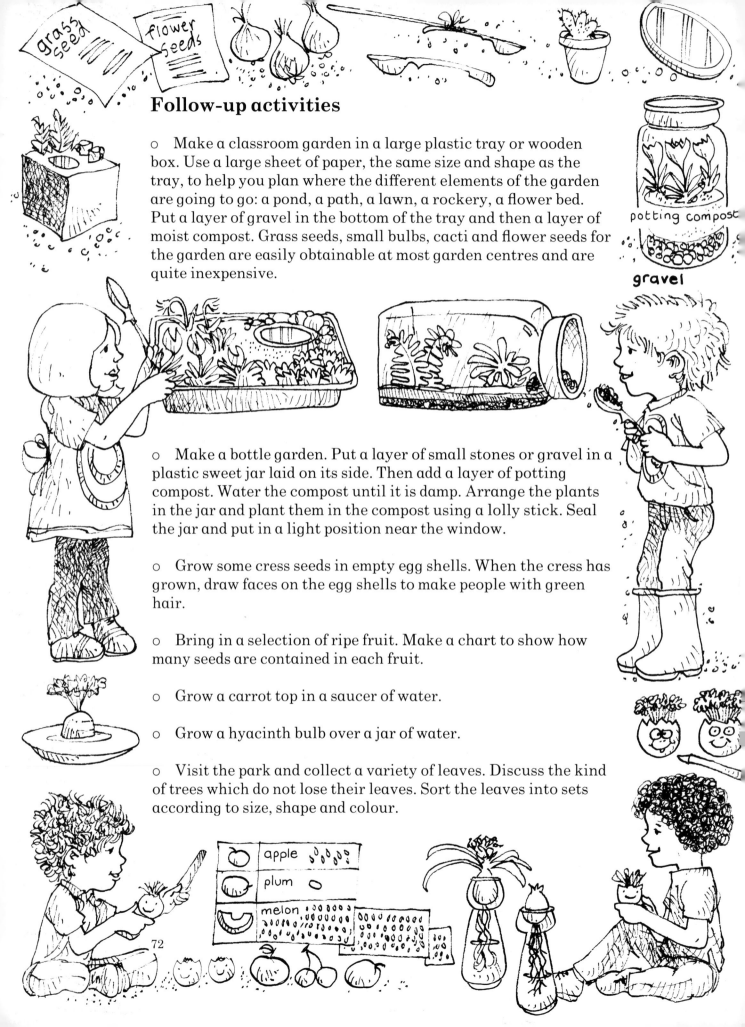

Follow-up activities

o   Make a classroom garden in a large plastic tray or wooden box. Use a large sheet of paper, the same size and shape as the tray, to help you plan where the different elements of the garden are going to go: a pond, a path, a lawn, a rockery, a flower bed. Put a layer of gravel in the bottom of the tray and then a layer of moist compost. Grass seeds, small bulbs, cacti and flower seeds for the garden are easily obtainable at most garden centres and are quite inexpensive.

potting compost

gravel

o   Make a bottle garden. Put a layer of small stones or gravel in a plastic sweet jar laid on its side. Then add a layer of potting compost. Water the compost until it is damp. Arrange the plants in the jar and plant them in the compost using a lolly stick. Seal the jar and put in a light position near the window.

o   Grow some cress seeds in empty egg shells. When the cress has grown, draw faces on the egg shells to make people with green hair.

o   Bring in a selection of ripe fruit. Make a chart to show how many seeds are contained in each fruit.

o   Grow a carrot top in a saucer of water.

o   Grow a hyacinth bulb over a jar of water.

o   Visit the park and collect a variety of leaves. Discuss the kind of trees which do not lose their leaves. Sort the leaves into sets according to size, shape and colour.

72

o   Paint the leaves and make leafprints. Match the colour of each leaf to the colour of your paints. Cut out the prints and make your own autumn tree display.

o   Make a scarecrow from old clothes bought cheaply at a jumble sale or donated by parents. Plant some bulbs in pots or gro-bags and leave your scarecrow to guard them from the birds.

o   Use powder paints to discover which two colours make green when they are mixed together.
   Investigate how many different shades of green can be made by mixing different quantities of paint together.
   Make individual forest pictures by putting blotches of the different greens on sugar paper with a sponge. Leave the paint to dry and then add black or brown tree trunks.

o   Play a counting and balancing game. Find two small, identical containers. Count how many conkers it takes to fill one of the containers. Then see how many acorns are needed to fill the second container. Which one holds the most/least? Why is this?

Now discover how many acorns it takes to balance five conkers.

o   Make potato prints.

o   Invent funny fruit and vegetable animals.

o   Make leaf rubbings.

o   Make bark rubbings.

o   Make attractive pictures and cards from pressed leaves and flowers.

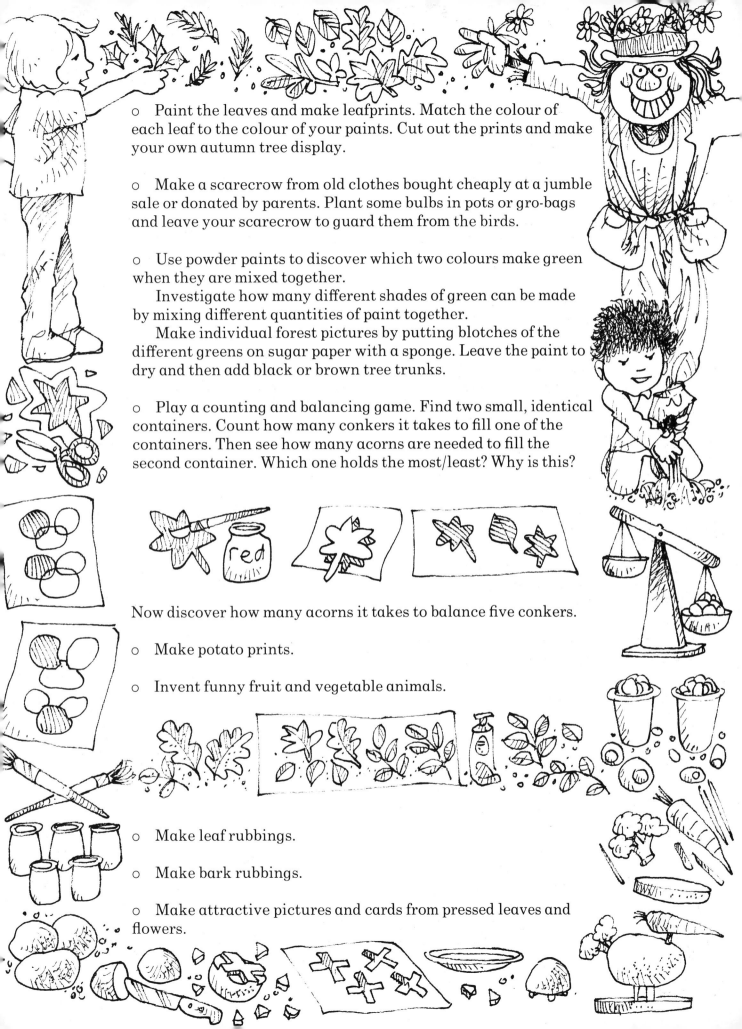

birds

Don't forget to feed the birds in winter   *Sandra Kerr*

1 You can for-get to leave your bike out in the rain   You can forget to drop your false teeth down the drain   You can forget to have a fright when you hear noi-ses in the night   But
DON'T FOR-GET TO FEED THE BIRDS IN WIN - TER!

You can forget to eat your chewing gum in bed
You can forget the monster in the garden shed
You can forget to leave a mess
Upon the floor when you undress
BUT DON'T FORGET TO FEED THE BIRDS IN WINTER

Every day be sure the garden birds are fed
And you can give them water with their daily bread
And in the summer you will see
Them flying high and flying free
IF YOU DON'T FORGET TO FEED THE BIRDS IN WINTER

Gran's bird cake
by Anne English

Andrew and Grandad were having their usual walk down the lane
behind the last row of houses. 'Can we stop and see the
blackbird's nest again?' Andrew asked, as they reached the
hedge.

Grandad lifted him up. 'The nest has been empty for a while,' he
said. 'The baby birds we watched growing up all summer are big
enough to fly away now.'

74

Andrew wanted to know where the birds had gone. Grandad waved his hand at the trees and bushes down the lane, then over at the houses and gardens. 'Not far away I expect. They'll stay where there is food for them – sensible things, birds.'

Grandad knew all about birds, which ones flew away for the winter and which ones lived here all year round. He knew all their names, and he was teaching them to Andrew. Already Andrew could recognize a sparrow, robin and the blue-tit.

Suddenly Grandad said, 'Hush,' and put his hand on Andrew's shoulder. 'Stand still a minute laddie, and look over at that hawthorn bush.' And there, pecking at the dark red berries, was a robin. He pecked and pecked until Andrew thought he would burst. 'It's greedy,' he said, as the robin flew away. 'Hungry, more likely,' said Grandad. 'No-one gives the birds three meals a day on a plate you know. They have to hunt for their food.'

'Like those red berries?' asked Andrew. Grandad nodded. 'Yes, and the big orange berries on the wild rose bush.'

'Rosehips,' said Andrew. 'And Gran says they eat the berries on her rowan tree – the very minute they're ripe.'

'They do that,' Grandad agreed. 'But they eat tiny insects and seeds too. And you've seen the blackbirds pulling worms out of the ground after rain. Finding food keeps them busy all day.'

They had reached the end of the lane and as they went through the creaky wooden gate that led back to the streets Grandad said, 'Now, when we get home you ask your Gran to tell you what she gives the birds in winter.'

Gran laughed when Andrew asked her. 'Your Grandad' she said. 'Him and his birds! Well, in winter I make the birds a bird cake.' Andrew had never heard of bird cake. 'Ah,' said Gran, 'it's a treat for them, I can tell you. You should see how many birds come down into the garden to eat it.'

'Sparrows and robins and blue-tits?' asked Andrew.

'And blackbirds and starlings and finches,' Gran chuckled. 'They all love my bird cake.' And she told Andrew how she made her bird cake.

'First I melt fat, like lard or dripping, in a container. An old basin or a used foil dish will do very well. Then I stir in small pieces of nuts, bacon, cheese scraps, crumbled-up brown bread, oatmeal and lentils. I leave them to set with the fat, then turn the cake out of the dish and put it out for the birds, either on the bird table or hanging up in the garden. Sometimes, for a special treat, I make my cake in a half coconut shell, and hang that out with the cake inside it. Next time I make my bird cake, you can help me,' Gran told Andrew, 'and you can watch all the birds have a special feast in the cold, wintry weather.'

Follow-up activities

o   Set up a bird table in view of a window and keep it supplied with food for the birds in winter: fat, suet, bones, cheese, unsalted nuts, oatmeal, sunflower seeds, bacon rind, dried fruit, apples, baked potatoes and tinned cat and dog food. Do not feed desiccated coconut, white bread or salted peanuts as these are all dangerous to birds. Always supply a bowl of fresh water. Keep a simple chart of the birds you see and the food they prefer.

o   Go on a mini-beast safari and see what animals you can discover in the leaf litter and under large rocks and rotting logs.

o   Make a 'Spider's Web' calendar. Use shiny wool or thread and sew through ready made holes.

o   Set up a wormery in an old aquarium and watch the worms at work in the soil.

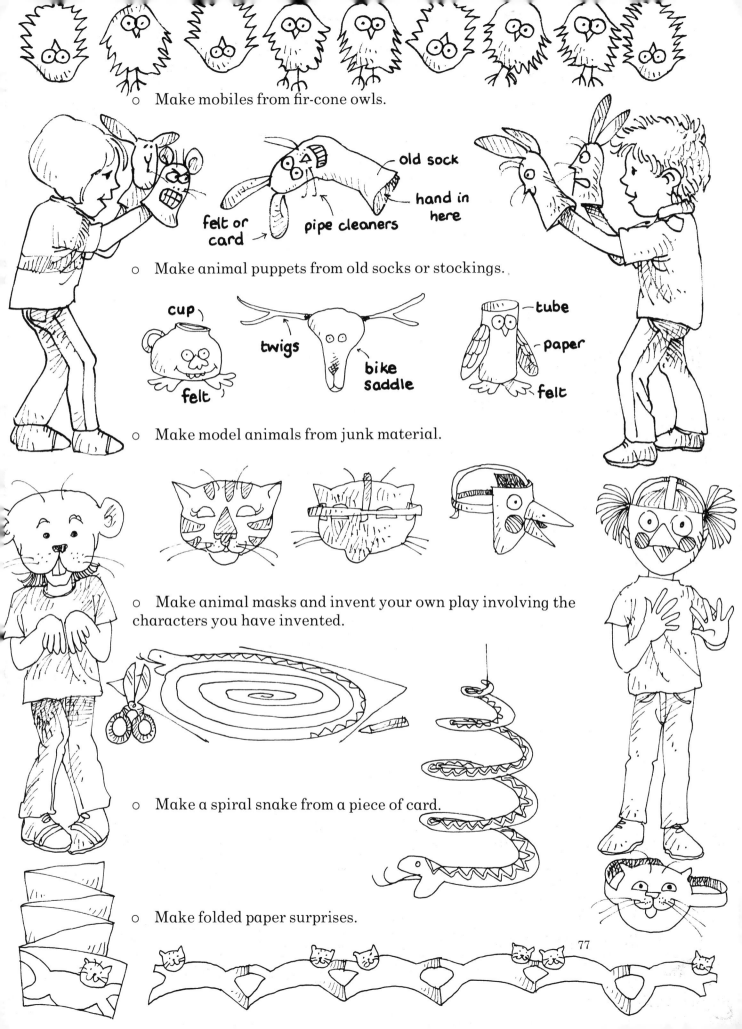

o   Make mobiles from fir-cone owls.

old sock

hand in here

felt or card

pipe cleaners

o   Make animal puppets from old socks or stockings.

cup

twigs

tube

paper

felt

bike saddle

felt

o   Make model animals from junk material.

o   Make animal masks and invent your own play involving the characters you have invented.

o   Make a spiral snake from a piece of card.

o   Make folded paper surprises.

77

spring

Cuckoo
by Guy Hutchins

Mr Blackbird flew back to his nest with a plump, juicy earwig.
'Goop-goop,' went the small pink chick as it swallowed it.

'Look, he's hungry,' said Mr Blackbird to his wife.

The next day he came back with two wriggly worms and a juicy
earwig. 'Goop-goop,' went the chick. It swallowed them all.

'I said he was hungry,' said Mr Blackbird.

'Goop-goop,' went the chick.

On the third day Mr Blackbird came back with three slimy
slugs; two wriggly worms – and an earwig. 'Goop-goop,' went the
chick. 'Perhaps he's got hiccups,' said his mother.

'I'm glad I remembered the earwig,' said Mr Blackbird. 'He's a
growing chick.'

The next day he brought four big, black beetles; three slimy
slugs; two wriggly worms – and an earwig. The chick swallowed
the lot. 'Look how fast he's growing,' said Mr Blackbird. 'Look –
he's as big as me.'

'Goop-goop,' went the chick.

On the fifth day Mr Blackbird came home with five fat flies;
four big, black beetles; three slimy slugs; two wriggly worms –
and an earwig. 'Eat up, son. It's the only way to grow big and
strong,' he said.

'Goop-goop,' went the chick.

'Perhaps it's the earwigs that give him hiccups,' said his
mother.

'But he likes them,' said Mr Blackbird.

On the sixth day he had to make several trips. There were six
creepy, crawly caterpillars; five fat flies; four big, black beetles;
three slimy slugs, and two wriggly worms.'

'Don't forget the earwig,' said Mrs Blackbird. 'You know how
he likes them.'

'They're getting quite hard to find,' said Mr Blackbird as he set
off again. When he came back the chick was so big he had to
stand on tiptoe to feed him.

'He's going to be a whopper,' said his wife proudly.

'Goop-goop,' said the chick.

'I'm worried about those hiccups,' said Mrs Blackbird.

'Guess what's for dinner today?' said Mr Blackbird on the seventh day. He stood on his wife's back and fed the chick seven sleek snails; six creepy, crawly caterpillars; five fat flies; four big, black beetles; three slimy slugs; two wriggly worms – and an earwig it had taken four hours to find.

'Goop-goop,' went the chick.

'He's going to be the biggest blackbird in the world,' said his mother. 'But I wish those hiccups would get better.'

On the eighth day Mr Blackbird got up especially early and was gone all day. 'I hope you're hungry,' he said when he came back. And he fed the chick eight wild woodlice, seven sleek snails; six creepy, crawly caterpillars; five fat flies; four big, black beetles; three slimy slugs, and two wriggly worms.

'Coo-coo,' went the chick. 'Where's the earwig?'

'I'm just going,' said Mr Blackbird.

On the ninth day it was almost dark as he huffed and puffed his way home. 'Have you got everything on the list?' said his wife.

'I think so. Nine greedy grubs – eight wild woodlice – seven sleek snails – six creepy, crawly caterpillars – five fat flies – four big, black beetles – three slimy slugs – two wriggly worms –'

'You haven't forgotten the earwig? You know he likes those.'

'It's in there somewhere,' said Mr Blackbird. He flopped down exhausted.

'Coo-coo,' went the chick. 'Coo-coo. Coo-coo.'

'There's something funny about that bird,' said Mr Blackbird. 'His voice reminds me of something.' And he went to sleep.

On the tenth day the moon was up when he came back.

'Ten squiggly spiders – nine greedy grubs – eight wild woodlice – seven sleek snails – six creepy, crawly caterpillars –'

'Coo-coo.'

'You're right. His voice *does* remind me of something,' said Mrs Blackbird.

' . . . five fat flies – four big, black beetles – three slimy snails – two wriggly worms – and an earwig.'

'Cuckoo! Cuckoo! Cuckoo!' went the chick.

And he swallowed the lot.

Follow-up activities

o   Find out more about festivals and celebrations which take place during the spring months: Shrove Tuesday, Easter, Holi Carnival, St Valentine's Day, St George's Day, and regional May Day celebrations such as the Padstow Hobby Horse Dance and the Kendal Egg Rolling Contest.

o   Make a zig-zag book of signs to show you spring is on the way.

o   Cook pancakes.
Pancake recipe
100 g plain flour
1 egg
1 pint of milk
1 tablespoon of melted butter

Method
Mix the flour, egg and milk together and whisk into a smooth batter. Pour a small amount of butter into a hot frying pan and add some of the batter. Cook for 2–3 minutes. Turn, or toss, the pancake and cook the other side. Serve immediately.

o   Have a pancake race.

Hot cross buns

Hot cross buns,
Hot cross buns,
One-a-penny, two-a-penny,
Hot cross buns.
If you have no daughters
Give them to your sons.
One-a-penny, two-a-penny,
Hot cross buns.

Traditional

80

o   Make hot cross buns.

Ingredients (to make 12 buns)

1 lb (450 g) flour	2 oz (60 g) currants
1 teaspoonful salt	1 oz (30 g) yeast
1 teaspoonful mixed spice	1½ oz (45 g) sugar
2 oz (60 g) butter	1 pint (250 ml) milk

Method

Preheat the oven to gas mark 7 (220°C, 425°F). Rub in the butter and add the currants. Mix the yeast and sugar together in a separate bowl and leave for a few minutes. Add the yeast mixture and milk to the flour mixture to form a dough. Beat the dough for about five minutes, cover with a cloth and leave in a warm place to rise for one hour. After the rising is complete, knead the dough for a further five minutes and divide into small portions. Roll each portion into a ball and mark each one with a cross. Return the buns to a warm place for a further 20 minutes to rise again. Bake for about 20 minutes and then glaze with milk and sugar mixture. Cool and eat

o   Make Easter cards.

o   Make a collection of different egg recipes.

o   Leave an Easter trail. Hard boil some white shelled eggs, with natural dyes such as onion (yellow) and beetroot (red). Allow them to cool and hide them around your house or garden for your family or friends to find.

More elaborate designs can be made by painting a pattern on each egg with melted wax before it is dyed and then scratching the wax off later to leave the design in white.

o   Read the story of the *Ugly Duckling*.

o   Make an 'Ugly Duckling' mobile.

o   Make a hobby horse with a broom, an old pillow case and some felt.

summer

I saw five birds

I saw five birds one summer's day
One summer's day, one summer's day
I saw five birds one summer's day
Perched on a sundial out to play.

The first decided to explore
He hopped away, and that left ... four.

I saw four birds ...

The second flew up in a tree,
Sat on her nest, and that left ... three.

I saw three birds ...

The third soared into the sky so blue,
Winged away, and that left ... two

I saw two birds ...

The fourth went off to sing a song,
And left the sundial with just ... one.

I saw one bird ...

She hopped off on to a stone
And left the sundial all alone.
Not quite alone, as you will see
For don't forget, there still was me!

Angela Garner

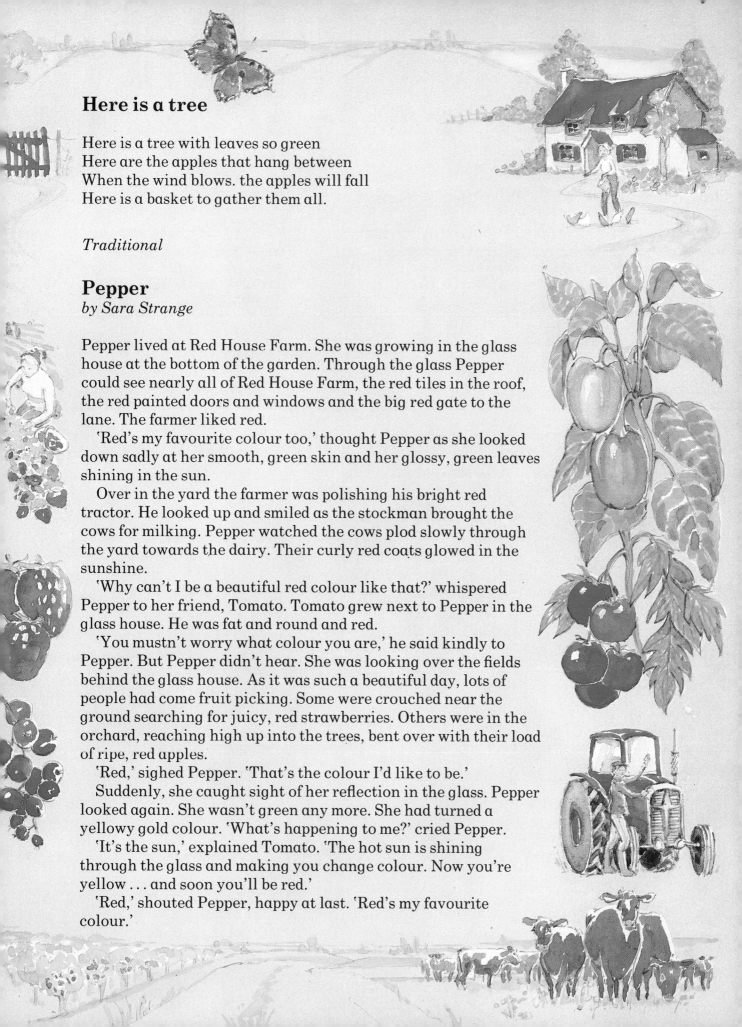

Here is a tree

Here is a tree with leaves so green
Here are the apples that hang between
When the wind blows. the apples will fall
Here is a basket to gather them all.

Traditional

Pepper
by Sara Strange

Pepper lived at Red House Farm. She was growing in the glass house at the bottom of the garden. Through the glass Pepper could see nearly all of Red House Farm, the red tiles in the roof, the red painted doors and windows and the big red gate to the lane. The farmer liked red.

'Red's my favourite colour too,' thought Pepper as she looked down sadly at her smooth, green skin and her glossy, green leaves shining in the sun.

Over in the yard the farmer was polishing his bright red tractor. He looked up and smiled as the stockman brought the cows for milking. Pepper watched the cows plod slowly through the yard towards the dairy. Their curly red coats glowed in the sunshine.

'Why can't I be a beautiful red colour like that?' whispered Pepper to her friend, Tomato. Tomato grew next to Pepper in the glass house. He was fat and round and red.

'You mustn't worry what colour you are,' he said kindly to Pepper. But Pepper didn't hear. She was looking over the fields behind the glass house. As it was such a beautiful day, lots of people had come fruit picking. Some were crouched near the ground searching for juicy, red strawberries. Others were in the orchard, reaching high up into the trees, bent over with their load of ripe, red apples.

'Red,' sighed Pepper. 'That's the colour I'd like to be.'

Suddenly, she caught sight of her reflection in the glass. Pepper looked again. She wasn't green any more. She had turned a yellowy gold colour. 'What's happening to me?' cried Pepper.

'It's the sun,' explained Tomato. 'The hot sun is shining through the glass and making you change colour. Now you're yellow . . . and soon you'll be red.'

'Red,' shouted Pepper, happy at last. 'Red's my favourite colour.'

Follow-up activities

o   The summer months are associated with light, warmth and a sense of well-being. Harvest festivals celebrate the completion of a successful harvest of various fruit, cereals and vegetables. Find out more about the different crops that are harvested during the summer and what happens to them once they leave the farm.

o   Make a plaited harvest loaf. Make a bread dough (various recipes are available), and knead the mixture until it is soft and pliable. Divide the dough into three equal amounts and roll into sausage-shaped lengths. Plait the strips and leave the dough to rise in a warm place. Brush with milk and bake in a hot oven for about half an hour, gas mark 8 (450°F, 230°C). Cool and serve.

o   Collect examples of the more common flowers and leaves to press. Lay the plants between sheets of blotting paper or paper towel and place several heavy books on top. After two weeks, the dried flowers can be arranged on folded paper or card to make invitations, wall hangings or birthday cards.

o   Experiment with various scented flowers to make perfume. Try stirring the petals in warm water or crush them with a little clear, light mineral oil, from a local chemist or health care shop.

o Go on a nature walk and look for examples of plants which are growing, plants in blossom and plants which have gone to seed.

o Collect examples of various cereals, grasses, flowers and seeds and glue them to stiff card. Make your design permanent by covering the plants with a clear, multi-purpose glue, such as PVC.

o Make a sunflower seed necklace.

o Make a sundial.

autumn

Fireworks

Ronald Zachary Taylor

1 Fire - works, fire - works what a pret - ty sight
2 There's a rock - et shoot - ing out of sight
3 Cath - 'rine wheels make cir - cles with a flash

Fly - ing in the air and light - ing up the night.
Leav - ing trails of star - dust red and gold and white.
Whoops! a Ro - man can - dle *Whiz! Bang! Crash!*
└─spoken

Chorus
Keep back! Don't touch! Stand quite clear

Let a grown-up light them and don't go near!

Magic stars

Magic stars going to the party,
Glitter trailing in the sky
A whirling loop the loop.
I'm coming too – rushing to the party,
Bubblebubble bibble bubble
Pumpkin soup!

Ann Bryant

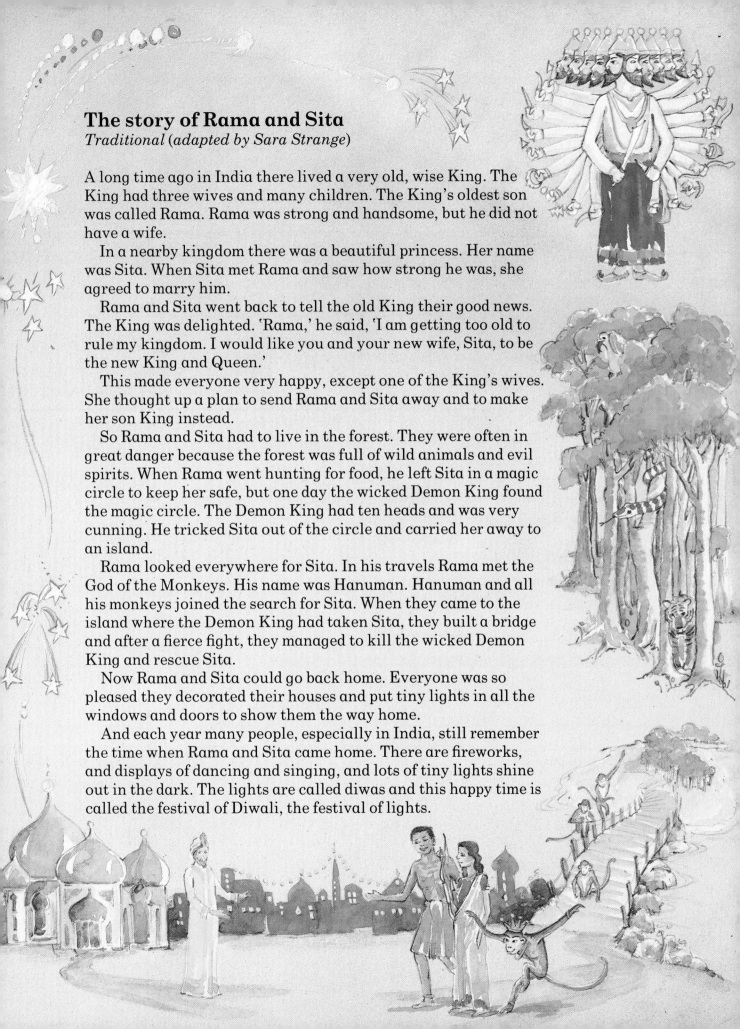

The story of Rama and Sita
Traditional (adapted by Sara Strange)

A long time ago in India there lived a very old, wise King. The King had three wives and many children. The King's oldest son was called Rama. Rama was strong and handsome, but he did not have a wife.

In a nearby kingdom there was a beautiful princess. Her name was Sita. When Sita met Rama and saw how strong he was, she agreed to marry him.

Rama and Sita went back to tell the old King their good news. The King was delighted. 'Rama,' he said, 'I am getting too old to rule my kingdom. I would like you and your new wife, Sita, to be the new King and Queen.'

This made everyone very happy, except one of the King's wives. She thought up a plan to send Rama and Sita away and to make her son King instead.

So Rama and Sita had to live in the forest. They were often in great danger because the forest was full of wild animals and evil spirits. When Rama went hunting for food, he left Sita in a magic circle to keep her safe, but one day the wicked Demon King found the magic circle. The Demon King had ten heads and was very cunning. He tricked Sita out of the circle and carried her away to an island.

Rama looked everywhere for Sita. In his travels Rama met the God of the Monkeys. His name was Hanuman. Hanuman and all his monkeys joined the search for Sita. When they came to the island where the Demon King had taken Sita, they built a bridge and after a fierce fight, they managed to kill the wicked Demon King and rescue Sita.

Now Rama and Sita could go back home. Everyone was so pleased they decorated their houses and put tiny lights in all the windows and doors to show them the way home.

And each year many people, especially in India, still remember the time when Rama and Sita came home. There are fireworks, and displays of dancing and singing, and lots of tiny lights shine out in the dark. The lights are called diwas and this happy time is called the festival of Diwali, the festival of lights.

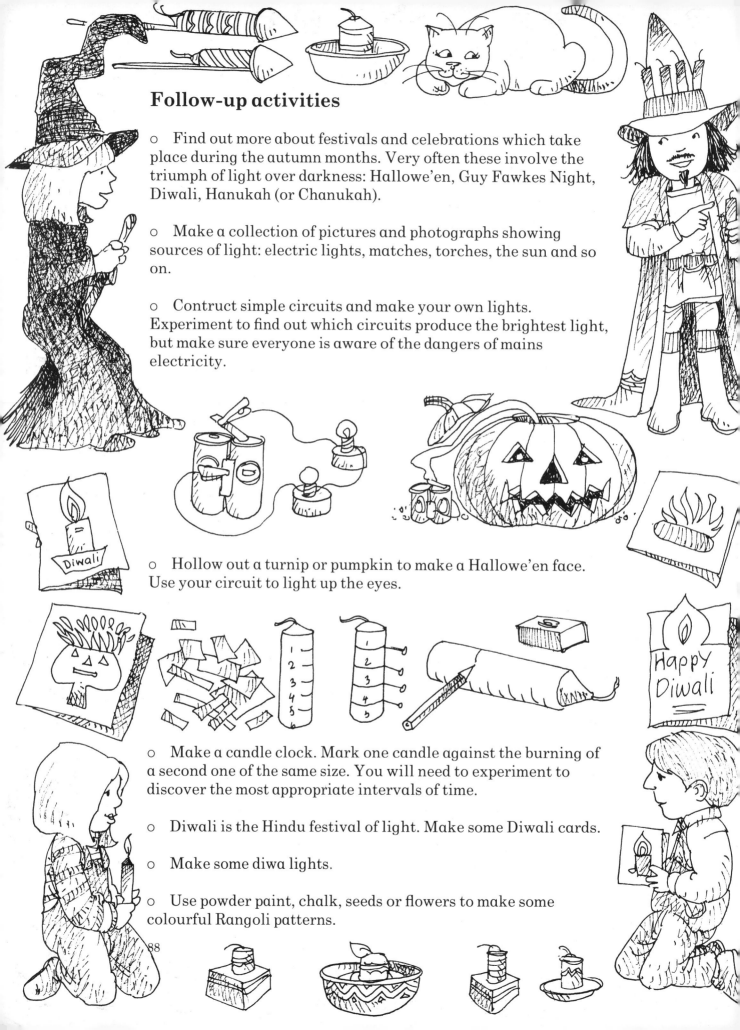

Follow-up activities

o   Find out more about festivals and celebrations which take place during the autumn months. Very often these involve the triumph of light over darkness: Hallowe'en, Guy Fawkes Night, Diwali, Hanukah (or Chanukah).

o   Make a collection of pictures and photographs showing sources of light: electric lights, matches, torches, the sun and so on.

o   Contruct simple circuits and make your own lights. Experiment to find out which circuits produce the brightest light, but make sure everyone is aware of the dangers of mains electricity.

o   Hollow out a turnip or pumpkin to make a Hallowe'en face. Use your circuit to light up the eyes.

o   Make a candle clock. Mark one candle against the burning of a second one of the same size. You will need to experiment to discover the most appropriate intervals of time.

o   Diwali is the Hindu festival of light. Make some Diwali cards.

o   Make some diwa lights.

o   Use powder paint, chalk, seeds or flowers to make some colourful Rangoli patterns.

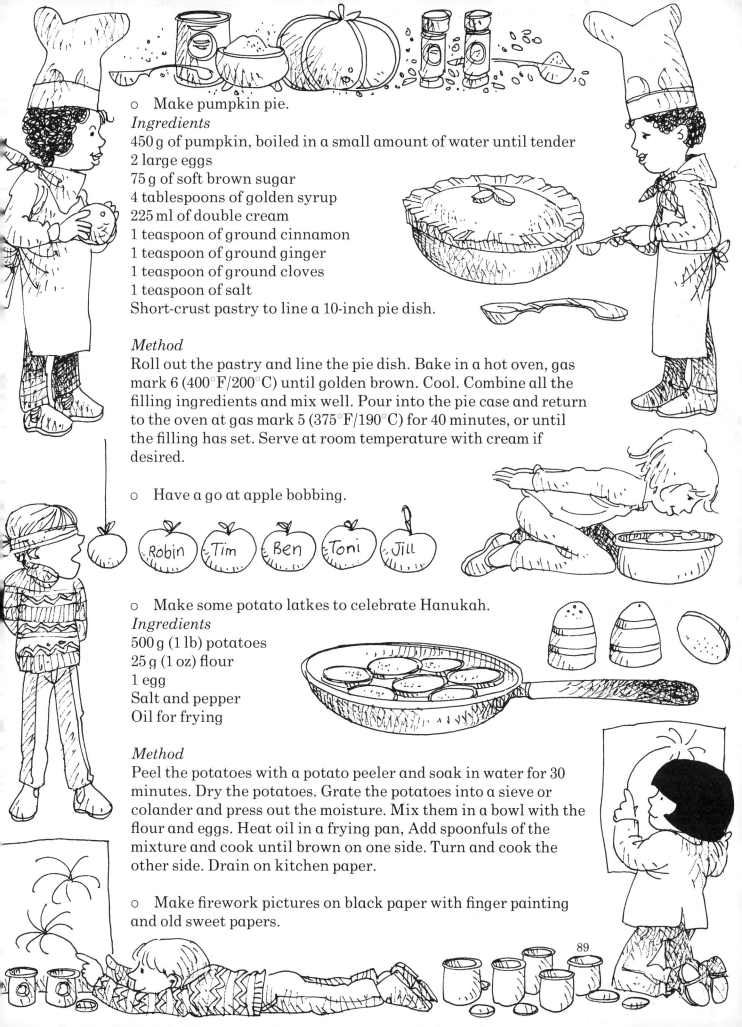

o   Make pumpkin pie.

Ingredients
450 g of pumpkin, boiled in a small amount of water until tender
2 large eggs
75 g of soft brown sugar
4 tablespoons of golden syrup
225 ml of double cream
1 teaspoon of ground cinnamon
1 teaspoon of ground ginger
1 teaspoon of ground cloves
1 teaspoon of salt
Short-crust pastry to line a 10-inch pie dish.

Method
Roll out the pastry and line the pie dish. Bake in a hot oven, gas mark 6 (400°F/200°C) until golden brown. Cool. Combine all the filling ingredients and mix well. Pour into the pie case and return to the oven at gas mark 5 (375°F/190°C) for 40 minutes, or until the filling has set. Serve at room temperature with cream if desired.

o   Have a go at apple bobbing.

Robin   Tim   Ben   Toni   Jill

o   Make some potato latkes to celebrate Hanukah.
Ingredients
500 g (1 lb) potatoes
25 g (1 oz) flour
1 egg
Salt and pepper
Oil for frying

Method
Peel the potatoes with a potato peeler and soak in water for 30 minutes. Dry the potatoes. Grate the potatoes into a sieve or colander and press out the moisture. Mix them in a bowl with the flour and eggs. Heat oil in a frying pan, Add spoonfuls of the mixture and cook until brown on one side. Turn and cook the other side. Drain on kitchen paper.

o   Make firework pictures on black paper with finger painting and old sweet papers.

89

winter

Three children sliding on the ice

Three children sliding on the ice
Upon a place which was too thin
That so at last it did fall out
That one of them fell in!

Two children sliding on the ice
Upon a place which was too thin
That so at last it did fall out
That one of them fell in!

One little child sliding on the ice
Upon a place which was too thin
That so at last it did fall out
That the last one fell in!

Joe Dunlop

The spiders' surprise
(adapted by Kate Wilkinson)

Once there was a mother and a father who wanted to make the
house shining clean for Christmas. Flick! Flick! went Dad with
the feather duster. Into the corners! Under the beds! Up over the
ceilings! Down the walls! Flick! Flick!

Vrmmmm-mmmm! went Mum with the vacuum cleaner,
gathering up all the dust and fluff. Vrmmmm-mmmm!

The spiders who lived in the house had a dreadful time trying to
hide from the vacuum cleaner and the feather duster. Skitter-
skitter! Off they scuttled as fast as they could behind the walls
and under the floorboards.

Not long before Christmas the mother and the father bought a
Christmas tree. Mum found some shiny baubles and tinkly bells
in a box under the stairs. Dad bought some chocolate shapes
wrapped in twists of silver paper and he carefully sprayed some

90

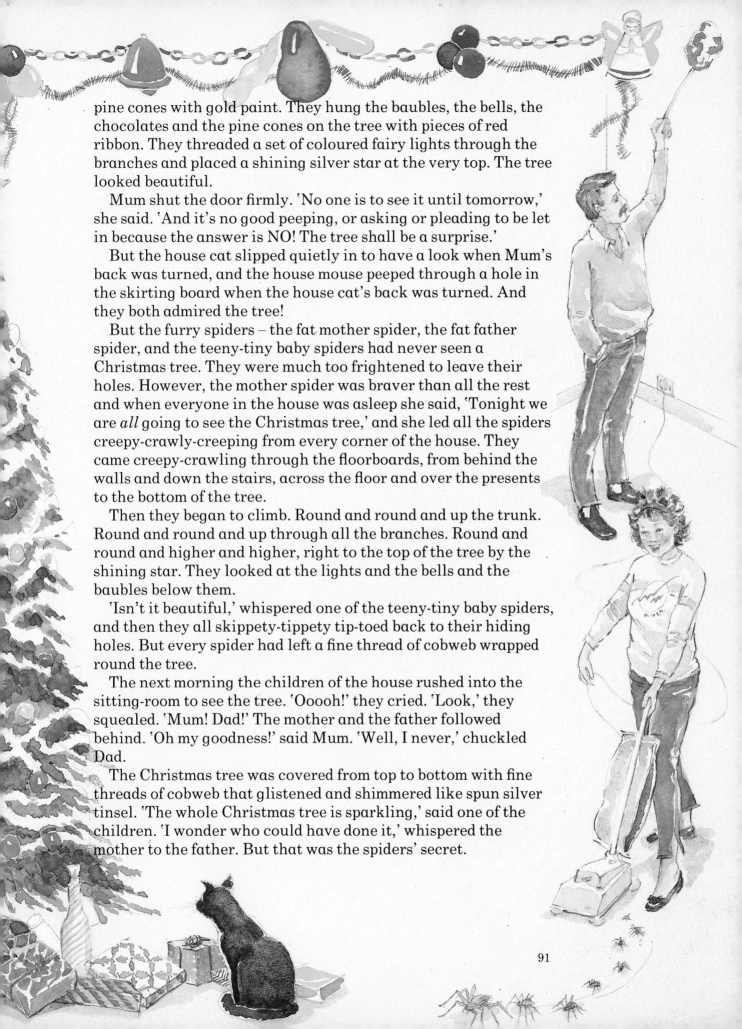

pine cones with gold paint. They hung the baubles, the bells, the chocolates and the pine cones on the tree with pieces of red ribbon. They threaded a set of coloured fairy lights through the branches and placed a shining silver star at the very top. The tree looked beautiful.

Mum shut the door firmly. 'No one is to see it until tomorrow,' she said. 'And it's no good peeping, or asking or pleading to be let in because the answer is NO! The tree shall be a surprise.'

But the house cat slipped quietly in to have a look when Mum's back was turned, and the house mouse peeped through a hole in the skirting board when the house cat's back was turned. And they both admired the tree!

But the furry spiders – the fat mother spider, the fat father spider, and the teeny-tiny baby spiders had never seen a Christmas tree. They were much too frightened to leave their holes. However, the mother spider was braver than all the rest and when everyone in the house was asleep she said, 'Tonight we are *all* going to see the Christmas tree,' and she led all the spiders creepy-crawly-creeping from every corner of the house. They came creepy-crawling through the floorboards, from behind the walls and down the stairs, across the floor and over the presents to the bottom of the tree.

Then they began to climb. Round and round and up the trunk. Round and round and up through all the branches. Round and round and higher and higher, right to the top of the tree by the shining star. They looked at the lights and the bells and the baubles below them.

'Isn't it beautiful,' whispered one of the teeny-tiny baby spiders, and then they all skippety-tippety tip-toed back to their hiding holes. But every spider had left a fine thread of cobweb wrapped round the tree.

The next morning the children of the house rushed into the sitting-room to see the tree. 'Ooooh!' they cried. 'Look,' they squealed. 'Mum! Dad!' The mother and the father followed behind. 'Oh my goodness!' said Mum. 'Well, I never,' chuckled Dad.

The Christmas tree was covered from top to bottom with fine threads of cobweb that glistened and shimmered like spun silver tinsel. 'The whole Christmas tree is sparkling,' said one of the children. 'I wonder who could have done it,' whispered the mother to the father. But that was the spiders' secret.

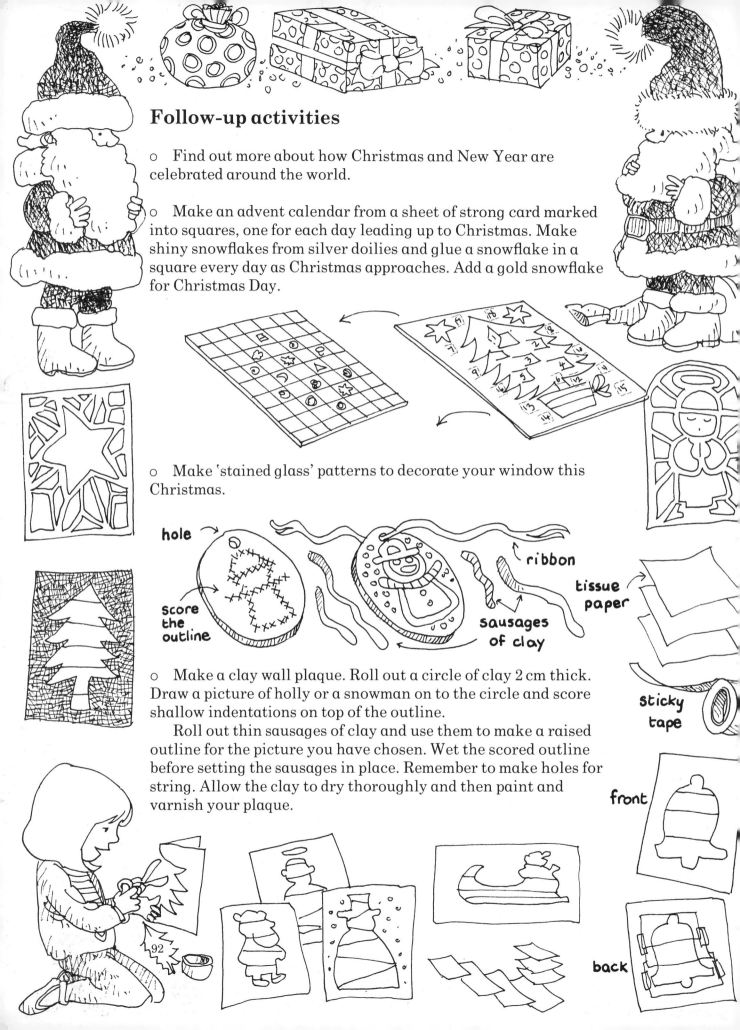

Follow-up activities

o   Find out more about how Christmas and New Year are celebrated around the world.

o   Make an advent calendar from a sheet of strong card marked into squares, one for each day leading up to Christmas. Make shiny snowflakes from silver doilies and glue a snowflake in a square every day as Christmas approaches. Add a gold snowflake for Christmas Day.

o   Make 'stained glass' patterns to decorate your window this Christmas.

o   Make a clay wall plaque. Roll out a circle of clay 2 cm thick. Draw a picture of holly or a snowman on to the circle and score shallow indentations on top of the outline.

Roll out thin sausages of clay and use them to make a raised outline for the picture you have chosen. Wet the scored outline before setting the sausages in place. Remember to make holes for string. Allow the clay to dry thoroughly and then paint and varnish your plaque.

hole

score
the
outline

ribbon

tissue
paper

sausages
of clay

sticky
tape

front

back

92

o Make a snowscene on a windowsill or in a large tray. Use tinfoil for the frozen pond. Cover the ground with a layer of cotton wool. Use pipe cleaners for skating figures. Paint houses and buildings on to thin card to make a background. Stick on people and trees with blue plasticine.

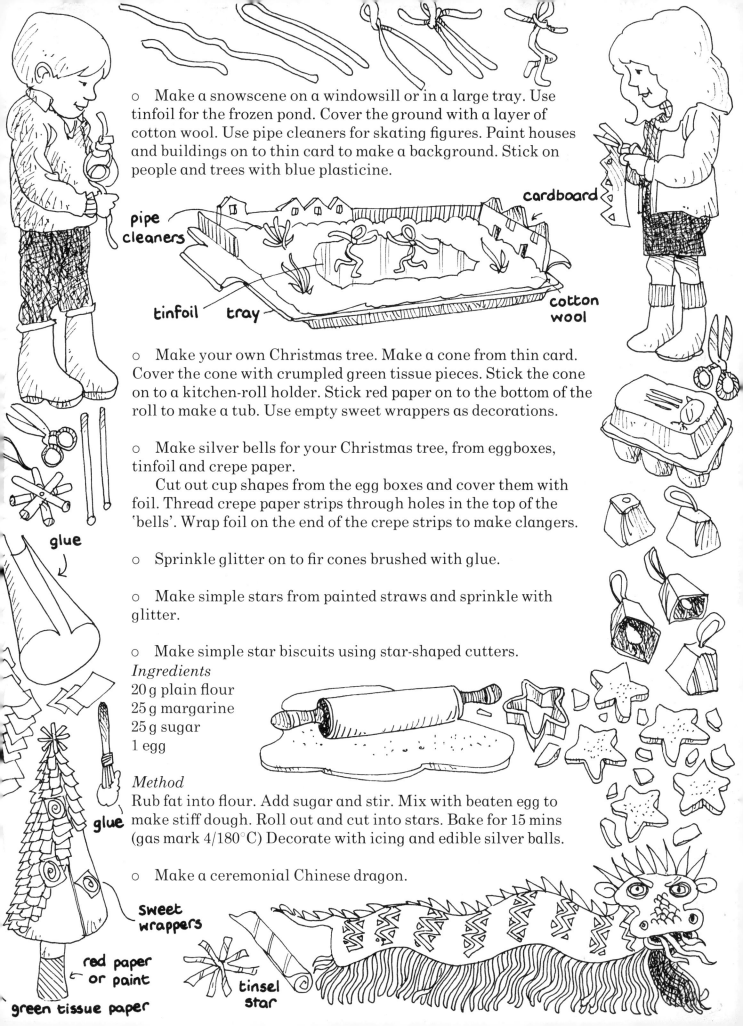

pipe cleaners

cardboard

tinfoil   tray

cotton wool

o Make your own Christmas tree. Make a cone from thin card. Cover the cone with crumpled green tissue pieces. Stick the cone on to a kitchen-roll holder. Stick red paper on to the bottom of the roll to make a tub. Use empty sweet wrappers as decorations.

o Make silver bells for your Christmas tree, from eggboxes, tinfoil and crepe paper.
Cut out cup shapes from the egg boxes and cover them with foil. Thread crepe paper strips through holes in the top of the 'bells'. Wrap foil on the end of the crepe strips to make clangers.

o Sprinkle glitter on to fir cones brushed with glue.

o Make simple stars from painted straws and sprinkle with glitter.

o Make simple star biscuits using star-shaped cutters.

Ingredients
20 g plain flour
25 g margarine
25 g sugar
1 egg

Method
Rub fat into flour. Add sugar and stir. Mix with beaten egg to make stiff dough. Roll out and cut into stars. Bake for 15 mins (gas mark 4/180°C) Decorate with icing and edible silver balls.

o Make a ceremonial Chinese dragon.

glue

glue

sweet wrappers

red paper or paint

green tissue paper

tinsel star

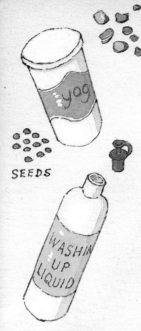
STONES

SEEDS

WASHING UP LIQUID

PASTA

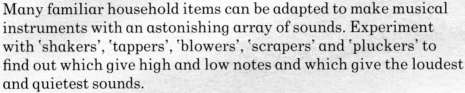

let's make music

Many familiar household items can be adapted to make musical instruments with an astonishing array of sounds. Experiment with 'shakers', 'tappers', 'blowers', 'scrapers' and 'pluckers' to find out which give high and low notes and which give the loudest and quietest sounds.

Have a go at accompanying your favourite songs or make up tunes of your own!

Shakers

o   Fill yoghurt pots and washing-up liquid bottles with seeds, pasta shapes or small stones to make shakers.

o   Make a paper plate tambourine.

o   Make a jingle stick.

o   Make a coat hanger shaker.

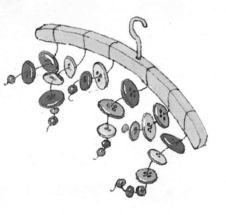

Tappers

o   Make a nail chime bar.
The nails can be substituted with lengths of bamboo, small flower pots, and so on.

o   Make stick castanets.

o   Bottles and glass jars of different shapes and sizes will give notes of different pitch. Experiment by adding small quantities of water to some containers.

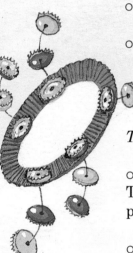

BISCUITS

P.B.

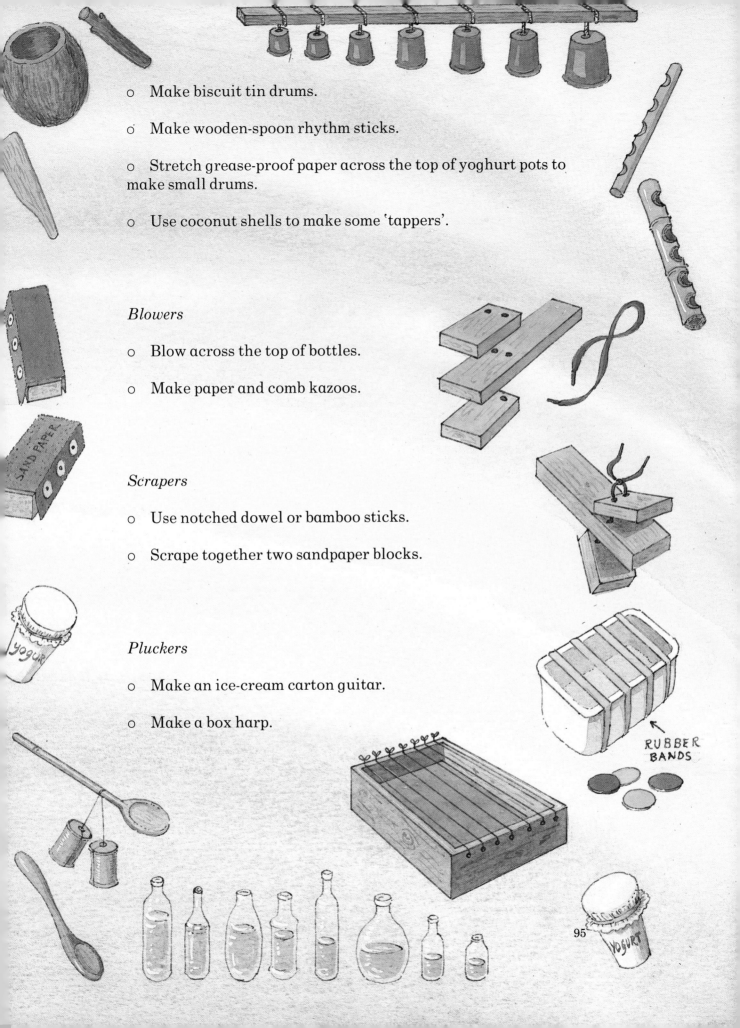

o Make biscuit tin drums.

o Make wooden-spoon rhythm sticks.

o Stretch grease-proof paper across the top of yoghurt pots to make small drums.

o Use coconut shells to make some 'tappers'.

Blowers

o Blow across the top of bottles.

o Make paper and comb kazoos.

Scrapers

o Use notched dowel or bamboo sticks.

o Scrape together two sandpaper blocks.

Pluckers

o Make an ice-cream carton guitar.

o Make a box harp.

RUBBER BANDS

95

acknowledgements

Acknowledgement is due to the following, whose permission is required for multiple reproduction:

ANNE ENGLISH for the words and ALISDAIR MACNEILL for the music 'The do-it-yourself song'; SANDRA KERR for 'Shake your hands, everybody' and 'Don't forget to feed the birds in winter'; JERRY O'REGAN for 'Chop, chop, chop'; RONALD ZACHARY TAYLOR for 'Fireworks', 'Water', 'I'm a little robot', 'How do you feel?', 'Our house', 'Don't be late' and 'Riding on my bike'; CHRIS WARDE for 'Going out to play'.

AUTHOR for 'The home-made bobby-dazzler' by Pam Ayres; FABER AND FABER LIMITED for 'John', taken from 'Let's Marry said the Cherry' by N M Bodecker; THE HAMLYN PUBLISHING GROUP for 'Choosing shoes' by Frida Wolfe; DAVID HIGHAM ASSOCIATES LIMITED for 'New Clothes for Old', taken from 'The Children's Bells' by Eleanor Farjeon, published by the Oxford University Press; CECILY WARE LITERARY AGENCY for 'The spider's surprise' by Kate Wilkinson.

The Publishers have made every attempt to trace the copyright holders, but in cases where they may have failed will be pleased to make the necessary arrangements at the first opportunity.

With thanks to the following for their illustrations:

Colour spreads
PRUE BERTHON for 'Let's pretend', 'Water', 'The sea', 'Weather' and 'Let's make music'; ELSA GODFREY for 'Growing things', 'Birds', 'Spring', 'Summer', 'Autumn' and 'Winter'; KATE SIMPSON for 'Hello, hello', 'This is me', 'Starting school', 'Food', 'Clothes' and 'Toys and games'; CHERYL TARBUCK for 'My house', 'My street', 'Tools and machines', 'Robots' and 'Transport'.

Black and white spreads
JULIET BREESE for all spreads up to and including 'Toys and games'; TONI GOFFE for the remaining spreads.